ALL THAT'S WRONG
WITH THE BIBLE:
CONTRADICTIONS,
ABSURDITIES, AND MORE

2nd *expanded edition*

A case-by-case presentation

Jonah David Conner

ISBN-13:978-1976427091
ISBN-10:1976427096

Preface to the 2nd expanded edition

As was to be expected, I received much feedback from Christians following the first publication of my book. Of all the criticism, there was one theme that stood out: something "went wrong" with me and that is why I left the faith. All the data presented was brushed off as a result of a personal crisis of some sort, such as a death in the family or a divorce. "Your decision was emotionally driven," they told me.

I have two responses to such an accusation. First, it is inevitable that strong feelings be present during any drastic change, but there is a great difference between emotions accompanying a change and emotions *causing* a change. The former was certainly true in my case, but the latter was not. No grave tragedy in my life caused me to leave the faith. My decision was due to the overwhelming evidence against Christian teachings, much of which I have clearly and honestly presented in this book.

Second, I wish to point out the fact that thousands of people convert to Christianity every year as a direct result of a personal crisis. On numerous occasions I have spoken with believers who told me they began to believe at their lowest point, when Jesus "reached out" to help them through that tough time. Why are Christians not condemning such conversions as "emotionally driven"? If my loss of faith is invalid because it was supposedly a result of personal difficulties, then all those conversions are equally so. We could just as reasonably conclude something "went wrong" that caused them to turn to religion.

THIS BOOK IS DEDICATED

TO ALL THOSE

WHO SEEK EVIDENCE

AND ARE WILLING

TO CHANGE THEIR MINDS.

"The best cure for Christianity
is reading the Bible."

—Mark Twain

"The Bible has driven reason from the
minds of millions. It has made credulity
the greatest of virtues, and investigation
the greatest of crimes. The instant we
admit that a book is too sacred to be
doubted or even reasoned about, we are
mental serfs."

"How long will mankind worship a
book? How long will it grovel in the dust
before the ignorant legends of the
barbaric past?"

—Robert Ingersoll

"Most of what discredits Christianity
comes from within Christianity.
You don't have to go outside
of religion to tear it apart."

—Dan Barker

TABLE OF CONTENTS

Introduction
Who am I to criticize the Bible?
What do I know? - 5

Chapter one: contradictions in the Bible - 9

1.1 Why do contradictions matter? - 11
1.2 Unfalsifiable inerrancy - 12
1.3 A word on the definition
        of contradiction - 18
1.4 Contradictions of names
        and numbers - 19
1.5 Contradictions of events and ideas - 29
1.6 Contradictions regarding the life,
        death, and resurrection of Jesus - 45

Chapter two: absurdities in the Bible - 60

2.1 Moral absurdities - 60
2.2 Theological absurdities - 77
2.3 Factual absurdities
        and exaggerations - 82

Chapter three: other problems with the Bible - 90

3.1 Bogus prophecies - 90
3.2 Repeated passages - 98
3.3 Scribal changes
        to the New Testament - 100
3.4 Sorting through the textual variants - 109

Conclusion - 114

*Bibliography and suggestions for further
reading* - 119

INTRODUCTION

WHO AM I TO CRITICIZE THE BIBLE?
WHAT DO I KNOW?

It is quite obvious to me that many people out there are more qualified to be writing something of this nature, and I make no attempt to present myself as any more advanced of a scholar than they are. That being said, it is equally true that I am no outsider to Christianity or biblical studies. Born into a conservative Protestant home and taught the Bible from an early age, I attended private Christian schools my entire childhood, from kindergarten to the end of my Bachelor's degree. One of my earliest memories from elementary school was being the fastest in my class to recite all 66 books of the Bible in order.

My religious indoctrination did not take a break in summer either, with Bible camps and other Christian activities such as Ken Ham's Answers in Genesis conferences, where speakers routinely claimed to have pictures of Noah's ark from the mountains of Turkey. Even my baseball league was run by Christians and would start every game with a devotional talk and prayer. On top of all this, I regularly attended church, normally two or three times per week, and remember daily reading the King James Bible by myself before school, eagerly underlining and commenting on my favorite verses. Everything I remember from my childhood revolved around Christianity.

Even after high school, my religious bubble remained intact. I completed a six-month training and missionary trip through the American Southwest with the organization Youth with a Mission (YWAM), based in Tyler, Texas. We traveled from city to city on a bus, sleeping anywhere we could (sometimes on the concrete floor of a church basement) while doing volunteer work and talking about the gospel to all who would listen. I distinctly recall going to the red-light district of Houston where a small group of us handed out tracts[1] to transgender prostitutes.

Shortly thereafter, I moved to the Northeast and completed a one-year certificate program at Word of Life Bible Institute. Located in rural Schroon Lake, New York, it was the closest I have ever been to life on a cult compound. Completely isolated from any secular influence, we were bathed 24 hours a day in the fundamentalist dogma of conservative Protestantism. As is to be expected, every single activity there had to do with the Bible. Every class was on the subject, every day we had obligatory "quiet time" in which we would read and pray, and everyone had to belong to a ministry team of some sort. The one I chose went on two trips to New York City to preach the gospel on the street corners of busy intersections. I am one of a small percentage in the world who can honestly say that they have preached on the streets of Manhattan. It is embarrassing to think about doing that today, but it was all normal activity at Word of Life Bible Institute. Anything like a traditional college experience was prohibited, including watching movies or listening to music in the dorms, and certainly any physical contact with the opposite gender. Ironically, however, it was there that I met my wife and we spent hours together canoeing on the lakes and local rivers, even though we were not supposed to do so

---

[1] A small pamphlet containing the basic gospel message on how to repent and be "saved."

unchaperoned. We have now been together for 15 years.

After my year in New York, I then transferred to Liberty University, Jerry Falwell's bastion of Christian fundamentalism, where I received a B.A. My academic focus there shifted and I and began to concentrate on Linguistics and Translation, specifically in regard to Spanish and Classical Greek, but also with other languages such as Portuguese, Latin, and Hebrew. I obtained an M.A. in Spanish from Northern Illinois University and wrote my thesis on Spanish Translation of the Greek New Testament. I later finished my Ph.D. in Linguistics with the Department of Spanish and Portuguese at the University of Wisconsin, with a minor in Classical Greek.

It was not until my late twenties that I began to question my beliefs. It was a slow process that took place over a period of about three years and involved detailed study of Textual Criticism,[2] Church History, Biology, Psychology, and other religions. For the first time, I read sacred texts of Hinduism, Buddhism, Islam, and other belief systems. Also vital during this period were the numerous intense conversations I had with both Christians and non-Christians alike. My goal was to learn as much as possible about these topics, something that continues to this day. One of the biggest issues during that time was the Scripture itself. Is it inerrant like all my pastors and teachers insisted? Did everything it says happened really happen? I slowly began to realize that the answer was a resounding "no." The results of my investigation led me to a drastic change in beliefs and resulted in my

---

[2] The study of biblical Hebrew and Greek manuscripts and the variant readings they contain.

leaving the faith. I now identify as an atheist.[3] It is safe to say, however, that religion has marked me for life and left a permanent effect on my view of humans and the universe.

The great irony is that the Bible itself was the biggest reason why I stopped believing the Bible. Comparative study of passages like the ones analyzed here made it undeniable that many of its claims were simply false. Time and time again it failed the test of reliability. My desire is that the contents of this book will aid others in seeing this as well.

My purpose, then, is twofold. First, I hope to open the eyes of the layman believer who has been taught that Scripture is perfect by ignorant or dishonest pastors and teachers. Second, I wish to provide a concise and informative resource for skeptics who do not come from a religious background but are interested in delving deeper into this important topic.

---

[3] Despite the many negative connotations associated with this term, it simply means "one who does not believe in any gods." Most atheists do not want to outlaw religion nor do they hate all believers. They simply view all gods in the way that Christians view Allah or Zeus.

CHAPTER ONE:
CONTRADICTIONS
IN THE BIBLE

Although the lists presented in this book are not meant to be exhaustive, each of the items has been researched individually and many possible solutions have been analyzed. These are the ones that have "made the cut," so to speak, since others of more questionable nature are not included here.[4] That being said, however, each entry is unique and some quite possibly have valid explanations that I have not considered. My work is not perfect and can certainly contain misunderstandings and mistakes. I am open-minded to hearing plausible arguments, and if I come across new evidence I have no problem taking one of these off the list or adding another to it. Feel free to contact me if you think one of these is unjustifiably included or if others should be here and are not. I will listen to anyone's honest opinion.

While the general public continues to be unaware of the existence of discrepancies in Scripture, nothing here is original with me nor will come as a surprise to any advanced Bible scholar. Every item presented has likely appeared in the work of someone else at some point in history. Some may seem like trifles, but if a god was really behind this, he or she could have made sure there were no factual inconsistencies and everything lined up flawlessly.

---

[4] Many more examples of contradictions can be found on www.infidels.org.

That would have been quite easy for an all-powerful deity who was trying to reveal himself or herself clearly and convincingly to humans. However, if many different men (and they most likely were all men) wrote, edited, and copied it in many different times and places, you would expect problems just like these.

Yet even if I am misled and plausible explanations exist for all of these contradictions, they at least prove that Scripture is not written as well as it could be. If humans can write something accurate and understandable, surely a god could do the same.

The following entries are presented in the order of which the first passage appears in the Bible as it is arranged today. In spite of the many divine names that are present throughout Scripture, I will here use only *Yahweh* for the sake of clarity and consistency. Due to the nature of this study, Yahweh is treated as a real entity. *I do not believe that such a god exists* or has ever existed. The verbiage used is done so for sake of argument.

In many of these I give an example of a common rebuttal, often from the very accessible and popular *Moody Bible Commentary*. These are meant to be representative of the mainstream interpretation of fundamentalists. Obviously I realize there are other opinions and not all are in agreement. My purpose in referencing this commentary is to show that if they admit a problem then there most assuredly is one, since they logically would try and avoid any negative presentation of their holy book.

1.1 WHY DO CONTRADICTIONS MATTER?

Scripturally speaking, I can think of few issues more significant than contradictions. The most obvious reason for this is that they give concrete evidence that at least some parts of the Bible *cannot* be true. And if some parts are not true, it cannot justifiably be presented as divine in origin, at least not from a god worth worshiping. The fundamentalists know this too, and that is why they fight this matter tooth and nail. Randall Price, a professor at Liberty University, proposes the following:

> [I]f this revelation can be claimed to be errant...it cannot maintain its status as divine revelation and becomes simply a man-made message. Consequently, if Scripture is not totally inerrant with reference to the things of this world, it has no authority to command men and has no claim above any other religious texts produced by mankind.

Mainstream Christianity has long held a similar view. It is no surprise, then, that so many ardently affirm the Bible to be perfectly and entirely trustworthy, even in its smallest detail. A clear example is found in this quote from Bob Wilkin, Executive Director of Grace Evangelical Society:

> The Bible is God's Word and is absolutely true in every detail. God never errs and neither

does His Word. God's Word is 100% true from Genesis to Revelation.⁵

This present book attempts to show how unfounded such a claim really is.

1.2 UNFALSIFIABLE INERRANCY

One of the most common defenses among evangelicals is that the problems we see today in the text represent scribal errors that corrupted the perfection of the original "inspired" manuscripts. There are a few significant problems with this claim, however. First and foremost is that *we have no original manuscripts of any kind*, not a single scrap of a single verse of a single book of the Bible. In fact, most manuscripts we have are from several centuries after the originals were likely composed, for both the Old and New Testaments.⁶ For instance, the oldest surviving copy of the Masoretic Text, the most authoritative source of the Hebrew OT, dates from the ninth century CE, well over 1,200 years after most of its contents were originally written.⁷ The Dead Sea Scrolls, earlier Hebrew manuscripts that date from around the first century BCE, improved this gap tremendously for some parts such as Isaiah and the

---

⁵ Both of these citations can be found on www.defendinginerrancy.com.
⁶ Throughout this book, Old Testament will be abbreviated as OT, and New Testament as NT.
⁷ I am not suggesting the Masoretic scribes produced poor quality work, quite the contrary. They were highly trained specialists with a passion for their literature. My argument is focused merely on the time gaps that undeniably exist.

Pentateuch, but numerous books are not present except in a few scraps of incomplete chapters. Christian pastors and teachers are regularly heard boasting about how all the OT is represented in the Dead Sea Scrolls, yet never go into detail about the actual representation, which is quite paltry indeed. For instance, the Scrolls contain much less than half of the modern text of Ruth, Job, Proverbs, Song of Solomon, Lamentations, Ezekiel, Daniel, and only a few verses of II Kings, I and II Chronicles, Ezra, Nehemiah, Hosea, Joel, Amos, Obadiah, Jonah, Micah, Nahum, Habakkuk, Zephaniah, Haggai, Zechariah, and Malachi. Esther is not represented at all.[8] To this day, the later Masoretic Text is the principal source for translations of the OT for this precise reason.

The NT fares much better as far as time gaps are concerned, but still is not nearly as impressive as it could be. The oldest complete gospel manuscripts in our possession are from around 200 CE, well over a century after they were likely composed and a full 170 years after Jesus is said to have been crucified. There are some fragments and even a few complete chapters before 200 CE, but that is all. The most complete and authoritative manuscripts (Codex Sinaiticus and Codex Vaticanus) date from the *fourth* century CE. It is common for evangelicals to brag about the large number of NT manuscripts that have survived, yet fail to mention that approximately 90 percent of them come from 800 CE or later.[9]

---

[8] Many online resources can verify this and a free digital view is available at www.deadseascrolls.org.
[9] All this has been well researched by numerous conservative and liberal scholars, most notably by Barbara

How can we then make any claim to the perfection of the originals when we do not actually have them? If the only manuscripts we have contain these contradictions, we have no basis whatsoever to claim that the originals did not contain them as well. For all we know, *they could have had more discrepancies* that were later smoothed out by the copyists. And even if the originals truly were perfect and the errors crept in at a later date, why was Yahweh able to inspire perfection in the beginning but could not oversee the copying process well enough to keep his revelation perfect for future generations? And if he is omniscient, why bother to inspire it perfectly if he knew it was not going to stay that way?

Another common defense of biblical contradictions is the idea that eyewitnesses were merely telling what they saw from different viewpoints and just because they do not all include the same details does not mean they disagree. It is true that merely telling something from a different perspective is not a contradiction, and omitting a particular detail is not either. The problem is that much more than a mere change of perspective is present in the Bible. If I tell you at the scene of a hit-and-run accident that the driver was an elderly man in a blue car and another witness says it was a teenager in a red truck, that does not constitute a mere difference of perspective; it is bad testimony. Someone does not know what they are talking about. Someone is simply wrong. Numerous instances of such clashing statements can be seen in the verses presented in this chapter.

Aland, Kurt Aland, Bart Ehrman, Bruce Metzger, and Daniel Wallace.

A related argument I have often heard is that the Scripture's multiple viewpoints (especially in the gospels) actually give it more credibility, and if they were all the same they would be accused of collaboration. I agree that more testimonies and more perspectives are good, but not when they disagree. It is actually very easy to give harmonious and unique testimonies that complement each other without conflicting. Going back to the hit-and-run analogy used above, if one eyewitness affirmed the driver was an elderly man in a blue car, and a second witness said he had white hair and was in a blue Toyota Camry, they would both collaborate and harmonize without contradicting. Nevertheless, this type of testimony is just not what we see in many parts of the Bible.

The great lengths that certain apologists go to in defending the Bible's inerrancy, if applied to other holy books, would render them perfect as well. Under their approach, the Upanishads, Bhaghavad Gita, Dhammapada, Koran, and Book of Mormon are also all perfect, and the Bible is therefore not unique. In fact, I doubt there is any book ever written that is not perfect if we try hard enough to come up with a solution for its discrepancies. One could write the most blatant contradiction possible in human language and there is some way that it could be reasoned away. For example, the statements "John Smith is an ugly, short man" and "John Smith is a handsome, tall man" would constitute a contradiction to any reasonable language user, yet these phrases could be said to represent a theological truth that goes beyond humans' superficial understanding. Thus "ugly" and "handsome" become spiritual symbols that are both equally true.

Of course, there are metaphors and symbols in every text, but with this extreme type of reasoning language becomes meaningless and a clear objective message is unattainable. *Such a method makes contradictions a complete impossibility.* This is what James McGrath, professor of Religion at Butler University, aptly refers to as "unfalsifiable inerrancy."[10] If there is no possibility of showing a true contradiction, then saying "the Bible has no contradictions" becomes an empty claim that could be said about every book, from the Koran to J.D. Salinger's *A Catcher in the Rye.* A confirmation of this would be to ask a religious conservative to give an example of two statements that actually would be contradictory if found in Scripture. Usually they will not do it, but if they do, it will be so outrageously detailed that it would never occur anywhere in any book.

What most surprises me about this class of apologists is they profess to care about what the Bible literally says yet do not actually care about what the Bible literally says. They reject evolution by natural selection based on what Genesis teaches about Yahweh creating the world in six days, yet when the Bible literally says Yahweh hated Ephraim and threatened to kill their children,[11] scriptural interpretation suddenly becomes quite metaphorical indeed.

I have heard and read numerous apologetic acrobatics done in an attempt to rule out the presence of contradictions in the Bible, by people who reiterate that there *must* be a solution "because the Bible is

---

[10] Taken from McGrath's blog on www.patheos.com, where many other thought-provoking writings can be found.
[11] Hosea 9:12-16. Ephraim was a tribe in ancient Israel, named after the second son of Joseph (Gen.48:1).

God's word and God cannot err" (Geisler and Howe 2008:11). Such an approach results in, as David Mills (2006:215) so rightly affirms, "Herculean, bend-over-backward, heel-behind-the-ear philosophical gymnastics" to make Scripture fit with reality. There is no way they will possibly admit there are true discrepancies, so they come up with the most fatuous and far-fetched explanations conceivable for conflicts of the most flagrant kind. This clearly indicates they are coming to Scripture with the a priori belief that it is perfect, which to me is unreasonable in the highest degree. If it is perfect, it should prove itself so *before* we believe it, yet modern apologists do it all completely backward. They first believe Scripture is inerrant then set about "proving" it.

Fundamentalists themselves even openly admit such bias. Time and time again, in numerous publications including William Lane Craig's *Reasonable Faith: Christian Truth and Apologetics*, they affirm that Scripture takes precedence over any other evidence. The organization Answers in Genesis repeatedly states "we must remember the Bible is never in error,"[12] which is the complete opposite of critical thinking. How any honest researcher could make such an assertion is beyond me. And how they can possibly deny a similar claim by Muslims or Mormons is an even greater mystery. Somehow Christians' prejudiced conclusions and circular reasonings are legitimate, but no one else's are.

If I were to present a similar list of discrepancies found in the Koran, evangelicals would not go to such great lengths to solve them and they certainly would not be convinced by the feeble explanations of Muslim apologists in regard to the

---

[12] See www.answersingenesis.org.

reliability of their holy book. They would simply conclude that the Koran was not trustworthy.

Obviously, one can do the opposite and come to the Bible looking for errors only to confirm an a priori belief that Christianity is false, and many have done that. This is not what happened, however, in my personal experience. These contradictions were studied and compiled *before* I left the faith, while I still believed that the Bible was divinely inspired. In fact, it was precisely these passages that were the most significant reason why I left Christianity. I went to Scripture looking to gain concrete evidence for my beliefs in order to better defend the faith, but what I found greatly disappointed me. It was shocking that I had never noticed most of them before, or that no one had ever mentioned them to me. I sat through hundreds of sermons and lectures about how wonderful the Bible was and how reliable its contents were, and never once did anyone suggest there were significant problems with the text, and certainly never gave me a list of such passages. I had to find out for myself the hard way.

1.3 A WORD ON THE DEFINITION OF CONTRADICTION

Merriam-Webster defines *contradiction* as "the act of saying something that is opposite or very different in meaning to something else; *a difference or disagreement between two things which means that both cannot be true*" (emphasis mine). It is in this sense that I use the term.

In the following lists, there are two basic types of contradictions. The first (type A) is the most basic and occurs simply when a latter phrase negates a former one or vice versa. The second (type B) occurs without negation but includes two phrases whose concepts are incompatible. Although it will be shown that there are true type A contradictions in the Bible, most of them are type B.

Type A: Simple negation.
        (X is Y. X is not Y.)

Examples: John is short. John is not short.
        John went to the park. John did not go to the park.

Type B: Incompatible characteristics or events.
        (X is Y. X is Z. [When Y ≠ Z].)

Examples: John is ugly. John is handsome.
        John was at the park at 7pm today.
        John was at the grocery store at 7pm today.

1.4 CONTRADICTIONS OF NAMES AND NUMBERS

1] Who was Selah's father?
Gen.11:12 Arphaxad was Selah's father. It specifically says Arphaxad was his father and that Selah was born when Arphaxad was 35.
Lk.3:35,36 Cainan was Selah's father. It specifically says Arphaxad was Selah's grandfather.

The classic fundamentalist rebuttal with these cases is to say that "father" just meant "ancestor" and Genesis just leaves out a generation. It is true that "father" can mean that, yet in this context it would not make any sense since both Genesis and Luke match every single name except Cainan. There is no reason why Genesis should skip only one generation, especially when giving such a detailed account that includes the exact ages when the children are born.

> Genesis 11:10-16: Noah > Shem > Arphaxad > Selah > Eber > Peleg.

> Luke 3:35,36: Noah > Shem > Arphaxad > *Cainan* > Selah > Eber > Peleg.

2] How old was Abraham when he left Haran?
Gen.11:26-32 Terah had Abraham when he was 70 years old. They moved to Haran and there Terah died at age 205 (i.e. Abraham lived 135 years in Haran).
Gen.12:4 Abraham was 75 when he left Haran.
Acts 7:4 Abraham did not leave Haran until after his father's death.

According to Acts 7:4, Abraham would have been 135 when he left Haran, but Genesis 12:4 specifically says he was 75. Some argue that Genesis 11 is not meant to be totally precise. However, it lists many proper names and ages with no round numbers: 304, 207, 34, 29, etc.

3] Who was Bashemath's father?
Gen.26:34 Bashemath's father was Elon the Hittite.
Gen.36:3 Bashemath's father was Ishmael.

These verses refer to the same woman, the wife of Esau. In fact, Genesis 36:3 even affirms that Elon the Hittite was the father of Esau's other wife Ada.

4] Who was Timnah?
Gen.36:12 Timnah was Eliphaz' concubine.

I Chr.1:36 Timnah was Eliphaz' son.

These come from two genealogical lists of Esau's descendants, so it cannot be argued that they are different people with the same name. *The Moody Bible Commentary*[13] even admits there is a problem, but blames it on scribal error.

5] How many generations were between Levi and Moses compared to those between Ephraim and Joshua?
Ex.6:16-20; I Chr.6:1-3; I Chr.23:12 Moses was *three* generations from Levi, even though there were supposedly about 400 years between them (Ex.12:40-41).
I Chr.7:20-27 Joshua, a contemporary of Moses, was *ten* generations from Ephraim, the nephew of Levi.

The conservative defense is that they "telescoped" the genealogies, only mentioning certain prominent figures. But why telescope for Moses in three separate lists, never giving the complete sequence of generations, but not do the same for Joshua, in the same books?

6] How many died in the plague?
Num.25:9 24,000 died in the plague.
I Cor.10:9 23,000 died in the plague.

I understand they are round numbers, but why not use the same round number for consistency's sake? Some have proposed that Numbers mentions

---

[13] *The Moody Bible Commentary* will be referred to throughout this book as simply "Moody."

total deaths, while I Corinthians mentions "in one day." The problem is Numbers just does not say that. It claims 24,000 people died in the plague and gives no implication that it was a prolonged affair. Discrepancies like these could have been quite easily resolved.

7] Where did Aaron die?
Num.33:38 Aaron died on Mt. Horeb.
Dt.10:6 Aaron died in Moshera (Mt. Horeb is not in Moshera).

While I hesitate to make claims about anything related to toponyms of the ancient world, the fact that Moody agrees and says the Deuteronomy passage is a later scribal interpolation is strong support for this being on the list.

8] Where did the Israelites go after Aaron's death?
Num.33:41,42 After Aaron's death, the Israelites went to Zalmonah and Punon.
Dt.10:6,7 After Aaron's death, the Israelites went to Gudgoah and Jothbath.

Again, toponyms can be unclear, but if these books were both written to give a detailed historical account, then there should be no problem being consistent with the terminology.

9] How many brothers did David have?
I Sam.16:10 David had seven brothers.
I Chr.2:13-15 David had six brothers.

Moody recognizes a problem here and suggests that one brother may have died young, so they left him out in Chronicles. However, in I Samuel 16 all were said to be *older* than David. Also, even if he died young, he obviously lived long enough to be mentioned in the I Samuel passage, so why not include him in I Chronicles?

10] Did David or Elhanan kill Goliath?
I Sam.17 David killed Goliath of Gath (a Gittite).
II Sam.21:19 Elhanan killed Goliath the Gittite.

A parallel passage in I Chronicles 20:5 claims that Elhanan killed the *brother* of Goliath, not Goliath himself. Because of this, some translations have "brother of" added to II Samuel 21:19 in an attempt to clarify the discrepancy. The problem is that the Masoretic Text (the most authoritative text of the original Hebrew) does not include these words in II Samuel. It is therefore possible that Goliath's death was attributed to David only after he became king and that Elhanan was really the one who killed him.[14]

11] Who was the high priest when David fled Saul?
I Sam.21:1-6 Ahimalek was the high priest.
Mk.2:26 Abiathar was the high priest.

Moody admits this is legitimate but blames the copyist. As I said before, there is no justification for such a claim since we have no original manuscripts and therefore do not know what they said. All manuscripts we have include this contradiction.

---

[14] For a more detailed discussion of this issue, see Baruch Halpern (2004).

12] How many horsemen did David take from Hadadezer?

II Sam.8:4   David took 1,700 horsemen from Hadadezer.
I Chr.18:4   David took 7,000 horsemen from Hadadezer.

In II Samuel 8:4, the Septuagint[15] says 7,000 horsemen, so some versions have inserted this in order to eliminate the error. However, the Masoretic text says 1,700, and that is how many versions read, including the King James and English Standard Version.

13] How many Syrian soldiers did David kill?

II Sam.10:18 David killed the men of 700 chariots.
I Chr.19:18 David killed the men of 7,000 chariots.

14] How many soldiers were there in Israel and Judah?

II Sam.24:9 There were 800,000 soldiers in Israel and 500,000 in Judah.
I Chr.21:5,6 There were 1,100,000 soldiers in Israel and 470,000 in Judah, even without counting Levi and Benjamin.

Some defend this stating that the II Samuel passage represents the numbers without counting Levi and Benjamin, while the I Chronicles passage refers to the total count. That is the exact *opposite* of what is said in the text, however, since it is I

---

[15] The Septuagint was the earliest Greek translation of the Hebrew Bible, likely done during the third and second centuries BCE. It is often used by Bible scholars to help shed light on the linguistic difficulties of ancient Hebrew.

Chronicles that says they did not count Levi and Benjamin. Even accepting that these are round numbers and overlooking the fact they are most likely exaggerated, there is a big difference between 1,100,000 and 800,000. 300,000 is an army in itself and would represent an enormous advantage in battle. Yahweh could have quite easily inspired them to use the same figures.

15] How many years was the famine supposed to last as punishment for David's census?
II Sam.24:13 The famine was to last seven years.
I Chr.21:12 The famine was to last three years.

The Septuagint reads "three" in both of these passages. Because of this, some translations like the English Standard Version have changed II Samuel to read "three" and thus eradicate the problem. Nonetheless, the Masoretic Text has "seven" here. They do, at least, include a footnote admitting this.

16] How much did David pay for the property he bought? Was it gold or silver?
II Sam.24:24 David paid 50 shekels of *silver* for the property.
I Chr.21:25 David paid 600 shekels of *gold* for the property.

17] How many stables did Solomon have?
I Kg.4:26 Solomon had 40,000 stables.
II Chr.9:25 Solomon had 4,000 stables.

18] How many governors did Solomon have?
I Kg.5:16 Solomon had 3,300 governors.
II Chr.2:2 Solomon had 3,600 governors.

Even if these are scribal mistakes, why would Yahweh not oversee that process as well? Why would perfection only be inspired at the beginning but not maintained in the transmission process? How do we know which verse is the true one?

19] How high were the columns of the temple?
I Kg.7:15 The columns were 18 cubits high.
II Chr.3:15 The columns were 35 cubits high.

These are not round numbers but exact measurements.

20] How many "baths" of water did the temple basin hold?
I Kg.7:26 The basin held 2,000 baths of water.
II Chr.4:5 The basin held 3,000 baths of water.

Despite being round numbers, they still represent a significant difference. A "bath" was about six gallons according to the English Standard Version translators, so the dissimilarity would be 6,000 gallons.

21] How many chief officers did Solomon have?
I Kg.9:23 Solomon had 550 chief officers.
II Chr.8:10 Solomon had 250 chief officers.

22] How many talents of gold were brought back from Ophir?
I Kg.9:28 420 talents of gold were brought back from Ophir.
II Chr.8:18 450 talents of gold were brought back from Ophir.

23] When did king Basha die?

I Kg.16:6-8 Basha died in the 26ᵗʰ year of Asa's reign.
II Chr.16:1 Basha attacked Judah in the 36ᵗʰ year of Asa's reign, ten years after I Kings claims he died.

24] When did the two kings named Joram begin to reign?

II Kg.1:17 Joram son of Ahab became king in the second year of Joram son of Jehosaphat. (In other words, Joram A became king two years after Joram B.)
II Kg.8:16 Joram son of Jehosaphat became king in the fifth year of Joram son of Ahab. (Joram B became king five years after Joram A, a confusing impossibility.)

Moody claims there was a co-regency, but the text does not mention it and would hardly reduce the conflict with dates and names.

25] How old was Ahaziah when he began to reign?

II Kg.8:26 Ahaziah was 22 when he began to reign.
II Chr.22:2 Ahaziah was 42 when he began to reign.

Moody again claims a possible co-regency but there is no textual support for this.

26] How old was Jehoachin when he began to reign?

II Kg.24:8 Jehoachin was 18 years old when he began to reign.
II Chr.36:9 Jehoachin was eight years old when he began to reign.

Moody even concedes II Chronicles to be an error of the Masoretic Text, since one Hebrew manuscript and the Greek Septuagint both say 18.

27] Who were Solomon's descendants?
I Chr.3:10-13 Solomon's descendants were Rehoboam > Abijah > Asa[ph] > Jehoshaphat > Joram > Ahaziah [also called Uzziah] > *Joash > Amaziah > Azariah* > Jotham...
Mt.1:8 Solomon's descendants were Rehoboam > Abijah > Asaph > Jehoshaphat > Joram > Uzziah > Jotham...

The writer of Matthew leaves out three whole generations, skipping straight from Uzziah to Jotham, then says there were "fourteen generations from David to the deportation." Obviously, for Matthew[16] the exact number was of importance, yet the figures he gives are simply false according to I Chronicles.

28] Who was Zechariah's father?
II Chr.24:20 Zechariah's father was Jehoida.
Mt.23:35 Zechariah's father was Barachiah.

Even if "father" just meant "ancestor," why the inconsistent names? Why list them at all if you are not going to do it accurately?

---

[16] Throughout this study, I will refer to the gospels by their traditional names for the sake of convenience. I do not endorse the belief that these texts were written by disciples or their colleagues. Even conservative scholars agree that *all four gospels were composed anonymously decades after the supposed events they narrate* and only afterward did the Church assign them the names Matthew, Mark, Luke, and John. We do not know who wrote them.

29] Who was Joseph's father?
Mt.1:16 Joseph's father was Jacob.
Lk.2:23 Joseph's father was Heli.

The data presented in Matthew and Luke disagree on many points. In fact, the genealogies are almost entirely different. The traditional explanation is that one is Mary's and the other is Joseph's, yet *both explicitly say they are Joseph's.* If it is Mary's, why would you not just say so, especially when you are claiming Joseph was not even Jesus' real father? What would be the point of a genealogy of someone you were not actually related to?

1.5 CONTRADICTIONS OF EVENTS AND IDEAS

1] Was the name "Yahweh" revealed to Abraham?
Gen.15:7,8 The name Yahweh (translated "the LORD") was revealed to Abraham and he used it to address him.
Ex.6:3 The name Yahweh was *not* revealed to Abraham.

The original Hebrew word is identical in these verses. It makes perfect sense when we realize that Genesis 15 and Exodus 6 were initially part of two separate documents that were later pieced together by an editor. It would make little sense if we say one author wrote the Pentateuch.[17]

---

[17] Both Jews and Christians have traditionally ascribed the Pentateuch (Genesis, Exodus, Leviticus, Numbers, and Deuteronomy) to Moses. There are many problems with

2] Did all the men of Sodom go to Lot's house?
Gen.19:4 "All of the men without exception, from young to old" went to Lot's house to accost the two angels.
Gen.19:12-14 Lot's two sons-in-law did not go to his house.

The writer here goes to great lengths in 19:4 to show that *every* male from Sodom was at Lot's house. The angels later told Lot to warn any more family members he had "in this city," so they would not be destroyed. He then went to talk to his sons-in-law, pleading with them to leave.

3] Does Yahweh tempt people?
II Sam.24:1 Yahweh tempted David to make a census.
Jam.1:13 Yahweh does *not* tempt anyone.

I understand there is overlap with the "test/tempt" idea, but II Samuel certainly refers to temptation to do evil, especially when we notice that the I Chronicles 21:1 parallel says *Satan* tempted David (see #18 of this section).

4] Has anyone seen Yahweh?
Gen.32:30; Ex.24:10-11; Is.6:1 Jacob, Moses, Aaron, 70 elders, and Isaiah all saw Yahweh.
Jn.1:18; I Tim.6:16 No one has or can see Yahweh.

The Hebrew word for "see" in all of these OT passages is the same. The Greek word in John and I Timothy is the exact word used in the Septuagint to

this claim, however. For a detailed explanation, see Friedman (1987).

translate the Hebrew in the passages above. Linguistically speaking, you could not be more contradictory if you tried.

5] Can someone see Yahweh's face and live?
Gen.32:30 Jacob saw Yahweh "face to face."
Ex.33:20 "No one can see Yahweh's face and live."

The Hebrew uses the same words for "see" and "face" in both these passages. Some evangelicals skirt the issue by suggesting the true essence of Yahweh cannot be seen because he is spirit, yet that is completely unjustifiable given what the text says.

6] Did all the Egyptian livestock die in plague six?
Ex.9:6 All the Egyptian livestock died in plague six.
Ex.9:25 All the Egyptian livestock did *not* die in plague six because they were hit with hail and fire in plague eight.
Ex.12:29 All the Egyptian livestock did *not* die in plague six because they lost their firstborns in plague ten.

Moody proposes that the Hebrew for "all" can mean "a lot," like the modern colloquial English "everybody." Yet if the text meant to say "a lot," the author(s) could have used a different Hebrew word to express that idea.

7] What are the Ten Commandments?
Ex.20 The traditional ten: keep the Sabbath, do not kill, do not steal, etc.
Ex.34 Seven of the ten are entirely different and include keeping the Festival of Weeks, not sacrificing

anything with yeast, and not cooking baby goats in their mother's milk.

Many apologists will defend this by claiming that one set is an ethical set and the other is a ritual set. The text does not permit this explanation, however, since the second set in Exodus 34 was said by Yahweh to be a *replacement* for the first set which Moses broke, and that on these new tablets he would write "the same thing as on the first tablets" (34:1). Yahweh then stated "on these I will establish my covenant with Israel" and that they were the "Ten Commandments" (34:27,28). *Most believers have never even heard of this.* Included here is a side-by-side comparison of the two separate lists:

(New International Version)

FIRST TEN COMMANDMENTS EX.20	SECOND TEN COMMANDMENTS EX.34
1] Do not have any other gods before me.	1] Do not worship any other god.
2] Do not make for yourself an image in the form of anything in heaven above or on the earth beneath or in the waters below.	2] Be careful not to make a treaty with those who live in the land.
3] Do not misuse the name of the Lord your God.	3] Do not make any idols.
4] Remember the Sabbath day by keeping it holy.	4] Celebrate the Festival of Unleavened Bread.

5] Honor your father and your mother.	5] The first offspring of every womb belongs to me, including all the firstborn males of your livestock, whether from herd or flock.
6] Do not kill.	6] Six days you shall labor, but on the seventh day you shall rest.
7] Do not commit adultery.	7] Celebrate the Festival of Weeks.
8] Do not steal.	8] Do not offer the blood of a sacrifice to me along with anything containing yeast, and do not let any of the sacrifice from the Passover Festival remain until morning.
9] Do not give false testimony against your neighbor.	9] Bring the best of the first fruits of your soil to the house of the Lord your God.
10] Do not covet your neighbor's house. Do not covet your neighbor's wife...or anything that belongs to your neighbor.	10] Do not cook a young goat in its mother's milk.

8] Should we make images of things?

Ex.20:4 "You shall *not* make any idol, nor any image of anything in heaven above or earth below."
Ex.25:18 "You shall make two cherubim of gold..."
Num.21:8,9 "Make a bronze snake and put it on a pole..."

Interestingly, the prohibition to make images is one of the first Ten Commandments, yet historically

Christians have ignored this and filled their churches with icons, statues, and figures of various kinds.

9] Are children punished for their fathers' sins?

Ex.20:5 "I am the Lord God...visiting the iniquity of the fathers upon the children unto the third and fourth generation..."

Dt.24:16 "No one will die for the sins of his father."

Dt.25:17-19 "Remember what the Amalekites did...they attacked you...wipe them out completely." (The Amalekite children could not have attacked Israel.)

Jos.8:24,25 Achan's entire family including sons and daughters were stoned to death because he took spoils from Jericho.

Ez.18:20 "No son will carry the guilt of his father."

Some assert the Ezekiel passage represents a later covenant, yet Deuteronomy also teaches that children are not punished, before Achan's family was killed in Joshua 8:24,25. Furthermore, different covenants would not represent a moral absolute, and Yahweh cannot therefore be presented as continually righteous or merciful.

10] Why was the Sabbath instituted?

Ex.20:11 The Sabbath was instituted to remember the divine rest after creation.

Dt.5:15 The Sabbath was instituted to remember the time enslaved in Egypt.

11] Does Yahweh dwell in houses built by men?

Ex.25:8 Yahweh told Moses that men should build him a tabernacle so that he could "dwell in their midst."

Acts 7:48; Acts 17:24 "God does not dwell in houses built by men."

Although Exodus was written in Hebrew and Acts in Greek, both words here mean "to reside, to dwell." There is thus still a contradiction of meaning despite not being the same original language.

12] Should we take revenge?
Num.31:1 Yahweh told Moses to take revenge on the Midianites.
Dt.25:17-19 Yahweh told Moses to take revenge on the Amalekites.
I Thess.5:15 "See that no one repays evil for evil, but always seek to do good to one another and to everyone."
I Pet.3:9 "Do not repay evil for evil."

13] Should we do good to those who hate us?
Dt.7:10 "Yahweh destroys those who hate him" and is quick to give them what they deserve.
Mt.6:44 "Love your enemies, do good to those who hate you."

Both #12 and #13 here represent only a few of the many inconsistent teachings between the OT and NT.

14] Is divorce acceptable?
Dt.24:1,2 A man can divorce his wife and remarry.
Mal.2:16 Yahweh hates divorce.
Mal.3:6 Yahweh does not change.
Mk.10:11-12 Jesus condemns divorce.

Jesus said it was allowed "because of the hardness of their hearts," which hardly characterizes a consistent moral statute. Some have argued that Deuteronomy represents a civil code necessary for Israel's social situation as a young nation. Even if this is so, I do not see why divorce would be allowed. If it is wrong, why not just tell the young nation that from the beginning?

15] Was Joshua alive when Hebron and Debir were conquered?
Jos.10:36-38 Joshua was alive and he participated in the battles.
Jud.1:1,10-13 Joshua was *not* alive and he did *not* participate in the battles.

Hebrew scholars Norman Gottwald (1999:153) and Christine Hayes (2012:191) both claim this is indeed a contradiction. It most likely occurs do to the nature of the OT compilation, which involved several sources edited by many scribes over time. One source likely claimed these two cities were conquered under Joshua, while another said they were conquered later. When the two texts were subsequently combined, these details were left unchanged.

16] When did Saul meet David and his father?
I Sam.16:19-23 Saul knew David and that Jesse was his father. Saul had regular contact with David.
I Sam.17:55-58 Saul did *not* know who David's father was and apparently did not know David really either.

At best, it is a badly ordered history; at worst, it is two conflicting stories about how and when Saul met David.

17] Did Michal have children?
II Sam.6:13 Michal was childless all her life.
II Sam.21:8 Michal had five sons.

Moody admits this is a discrepancy. They also affirm that the ancients recognized it and certain scribes changed the name to Merab, Michal's sister in II Samuel 21.

18] Who tempted David to take a census?
II Sam.24:1 *Yahweh* tempted David to take a census.
I Chr.21:1 *Satan* tempted David to take a census.

The Hebrew word for "tempt" is the exact same in both verses. Not only is there the obvious contradiction between Yahweh and Satan, there is also the absurdity of Yahweh inciting David to do something he later punished him for.

19] Did Asa take away the high places of worship?
I Kg.15:14 Asa did *not* take away the high places.
II Chr.14:2,3 Asa did take away the high places.

20] Does Yahweh lie and deceive?
I Kg.22:19-23 Yahweh approved of the lying angel and sent him to Ahab.
Jn.17:17 Yahweh's word is truth.
II Thess.2:11 Yahweh actively will send a delusion in order to deceive people.
Tit.1:2 Yahweh cannot lie.

21] Are all rulers established by Yahweh?

Hos.8:3,4 "Israel...establishes kings that I do not approve of, and they chose authorities that I do not know."
Rom.13:1 "There is no authority except that which God has established. The authorities that exist have been established by God."

22] Should we hate people?
Hos.9:12-16 Yahweh said he hated Ephraim.
Mal.1:3; Rom.9:11-18 Yahweh hated Esau.
I Jn.3:15 "Whoever hates his brother is a murderer, and you know that no murderer has eternal life abiding in him."

The Greek word used here in Romans and I John is the most common word for "hate." I have personally heard pastors preach that the Romans verse means "to love less" or "to not choose," but there is absolutely no linguistic justification for such a claim. The same word here appears 40 times in the NT and every single time is translated "hate," including Luke 6:22 and John 15:25.

23] Had the ruler's daughter died or was she just really sick?
Mt.9:18 The ruler told Jesus "my daughter has just died."
Mk.5:23,35; Lk.8:42 The ruler told Jesus that his daughter was sick and close to dying.

All three gospels end up with the daughter being dead, but the contradiction is with what was initially said. I think most people would agree there is a pretty significant difference between being very ill and dead.

24] Did a messenger come to tell the ruler his daughter had just died?
Mt.9:18 The ruler himself told Jesus "my daughter has just died." No messenger came later.
Mk.5:23,35; Lk.8:42 While the ruler was talking with Jesus, a messenger came and told him his daughter had died.

25] Why could the disciples not cast out the demon?
Mt.17:20 The disciples could not cast out the demon "because of their little faith."
Mk.9:29 The disciples could not cast out the demon because that class of demon could "only be cast out by prayer and fasting."

Strong support for this being a contradiction is the fact that, in some manuscripts, scribes noticed it and added Mark's phrase to Matthew as a separate verse in 17:21.[18] Most modern translations have rectified this and now do not even include 17:21 in Matthew, or they put it as a footnote.

26] Who asked for James and John to sit at Jesus' right and left hand in his kingdom?
Mt.20:20 The *mother* of James and John went with them and she asked Jesus to let her sons sit on his right and left.
Mk.10:35 James and John asked for themselves. Their mother is not even mentioned.

27] When did the disciples notice the withered fig tree?

---

[18] See section 3.3 for more examples of scribal changes to the text.

Mt.21:19,20   The disciples were immediately amazed at the withered fig tree.
Mk.11:20,21   The disciples did not notice the withered fig tree until the next day.

28] How many times was the rooster going to crow before Peter's denial?
Mt.26:34 Peter was going to deny Christ before the rooster crowed (i.e. before it crowed once).
Mk.14:30 Peter was going to deny Christ before the rooster crowed *twice*.

29] Who did Peter talk to when he denied Christ the *second* time?
Mt.26:71,72 A *girl* addressed Peter and he responded to her.
Lk.22:58 A *man* addressed Peter and he responded to him. His *first* denial was to a young girl.

Some have defended this by pointing out that multiple people were gathered around. This is correct according to the context but the disagreement is found in that Matthew distinctly states a girl addressed Peter the second time, while Luke declares it was a man. In fact, after affirming that Peter's *first* denial was to a girl, Luke specifically says "someone else" addressed Peter the second time. Consequently, whether there was a group there or not is irrelevant.

30] Who bought the field with money from Jesus' betrayal?
Mt.27:6,7 The priests bought the field.
Acts 1:16-19 Judas bought the field.

Moody denies a contradiction in this particular case by proposing that the priests bought it with Judas' money, so technically Judas bought it. Like with other passages presented here, such an explanation is found nowhere in the text itself and is purely speculative. Even if it were true, the biblical writers have still failed to give clear and consistent testimony.

31] Why was the field called "field of blood"?
Mt.27:7 The field was called "field of blood" because it was bought with blood money.
Acts 1:11 The field was called "field of blood" because Judas died there, with his guts bursting out.

To harmonize passages like this, many apologists will simply assert that both are true. Such a defense is hardly convincing and demonstrates yet another case of the interpretative gymnastics that they must do to make sense of these kinds of verses.

32] When did Satan enter Judas?
Lk.22:1-7 Satan entered Judas *before* the Passover meal.
Jn.13:27 Satan entered Judas specifically *during* the Passover meal, the instant when Judas took the bread.

Some maintain that Satan was coming and going in and out of Judas, but no gospel suggests this at all. Both Luke and John only mention one time when Satan supposedly entered him.

33] Where did Paul go immediately after his conversion?
Acts 9:1-22 After his conversion, Paul went immediately to the synagogues of Damascus to preach the gospel.

Gal.1:15-17 After his conversion, Paul went immediately to Arabia before returning to Damascus.

Acts contains much biographical information about Paul (or Saul) of Tarsus, yet was not written by him. Since most scholars agree Paul did in fact write Galatians, it is reasonable to think he would more accurately recount the events of his own life rather than someone else. Out of the two accounts, the latter is therefore the most likely to be correct.

34] Did the witnesses to Paul's conversion stand or fall down?
Acts 9:7 The witnesses stood speechless.
Acts 26:14 The witnesses all fell down.

Although the Greek verb translated "stood" in 9:7 can at times be interpreted as "stayed" or "remained," by far the most common definition is "stand" and it is the only one that really fits the context. Strong evidence for this is that virtually every authoritative translation reads "stood" in 9:7. Others propose that the men first fell down and then stood up, but that is pure conjecture since neither passage suggests that at all.

35] Did the witnesses to Paul's conversion hear anything?
Acts 9:7 The witnesses heard a voice.
Acts 22:9 The witnesses did *not* hear a voice.

The Greek terms for "hear" and "voice" are the same in both phrases. Some dishonestly translate 22:9 as "did not understand," but there are many arguments against this, the main one being the fact that it is the exact same word in the exact same context. There are other Greek words that Luke could have used if he wanted to say "understand." See Barker (2008:243-250) for a more detailed analysis of this passage.

36] Does Yahweh show favoritism?
Rom.2:11 Yahweh does *not* show favoritism.
Rom.9:12-18 Yahweh shows favoritism.

To make matters worse, certain passages such as James 2:8,9 claim that showing favoritism is a sin, yet that is exactly what they affirm Yahweh did throughout most of history.

To me it never made sense why a god would choose one people group for anything at all. Why would he or she not reveal the same message to everyone in all times and places? I have never heard a convincing answer for this. There is no way to get around the fact that millions of people across space and time have lived and died without hearing a word about Yahweh or Jesus. How can Christians possibly claim their God cares about everyone equally? However, when we realize the Bible was written by Israelites, it makes perfect sense why they would say Yahweh chose Israel. Every people group thinks they are special in some way, and the ancients were no exception.

37] Is Abraham an example of salvation through faith alone?
Rom.4 Abraham is an example of salvation through faith alone. He was justified even before he was circumcised.
Jam.2:21-24 Abraham is *not* an example of salvation through faith alone. He was also justified by his actions.

The fact that the book of James was controversial in being accepted into the canon and that later prominent theologians such as Martin Luther had serious doubts about its validity shows that something is clearly wrong here.

38] Are we justified by works?
Gal.2:16 "A man is *not* justified by works of the law but by faith."
Jam.2:24 "By works a man is justified, not by faith only."

The Greek words translated "faith," "works," and "justified" are the same here in both passages. Furthermore, they are almost mirror opposites in their phrasing. In order to make them harmonize, some fundamentalists attempt to differentiate between "works of the law" in Galatians and only "works" in James. Throughout Paul's epistles, however, it is openly taught that salvation does not come through any works at all but through faith only, so regardless of what type of works James is referring to he openly conflicts with Paul.

39] Is it alright to swear (make an oath)?
Heb.6:13 Yahweh swore to Abraham.
Jam.5:12 "Do not swear, either by heaven or by earth."

This would seem petty were it not for the fact that the Greek word for "swear" is the same in both passages. This is a clear case of Yahweh not practicing what he preaches.

1.6 CONTRADICTIONS REGARDING THE LIFE, DEATH, AND RESURRECTION OF JESUS

One of the most shocking studies I have ever done with the Bible was a parallel comparison of the birth, crucifixion, and resurrection accounts. Supposedly being the most significant events in the history of humanity, I expected to see everything totally lined up with detailed agreement. That is unquestionably not the case. One would think this would be the time Yahweh would most want to be precise and transparent, but that simply does not happen.

David Hume, the famous Scottish philosopher of the 18th century, declared in his *Enquiry Concerning Human Understanding* (1748)[19] that it was reasonable to doubt a testimony if:

1] There are few witnesses of the event.
2] The witnesses disagree.
3] The witnesses benefit from their testimony being true.

All three of these apply in many instances concerning Jesus. As the examples will demonstrate, the overall differences are quite jarring indeed, especially with the resurrection narrative. They are so distinct from each other that it amazes me they have persuaded so many people for so long. Any reasonable and objective evaluation forces us to admit the following is neither consistent nor reliable testimony. It would hardly serve to convince even if the content

---

[19] See the 2013 reprint, pages 50-60.

were not miraculous, much less when we consider the extraordinary message it contains.

For sake of logical flow, the items are presented according to the general chronology of events, rather than arrangement in the NT.

1] How many generations were between Jesus and David?

Mt.1:1-17 There were 28 generations between Jesus and David.

Lk.3:23-38 There were 43 generations between Jesus and David.

Some say Matthew's gospel just skipped some generations on purpose, but why would he do that if his goal was to give a detailed account of Christ's lineage? Skipping fifteen generations is not exactly a convincing method. Again, why list any genealogy at all if he is not going to do it accurately?

2] Were there 41 or 42 generations between Abraham and Jesus?

Mt.1:1-17 Matthew claims there were three sets of fourteen generations between Abraham and Jesus, (totaling 42) yet only 41 generations are listed.

Moody defends this by maintaining that David was counted twice. This is possible since he is mentioned two times in 1:17, yet this would still be a mistake, since overall it would end up being one generation short from the 42 total generations between Abraham and Christ. One man cannot constitute two generations, regardless of who he is.

3] Where did Joseph and Mary go after Jesus' birth in Bethlehem?

Mt.2:13-23 Joseph and Mary went from Bethlehem *directly to Egypt*, and stayed there a while before relocating to Galilee.
Lk.2:21-39 Joseph and Mary went from Bethlehem to *Jerusalem* for circumcision then directly *back to Galilee* after "the time of purification," about a month. There is no mention of any flight to Egypt.

The most common rebuttal here among fundamentalists is that Luke merely omitted the flight to Egypt, which occurred after they went back to Galilee. However, that would still conflict with Matthew's claim that they went directly to Egypt from Bethlehem, which is not in Galilee.[20]

Overall, both authors paint a very different picture of the birth narrative. Matthew starts out with Jesus being born in Bethlehem, even claiming in 2:11 that they had a *house* there (the Greek word is the most common term for "house" or "home"), which would mean *they originally lived in Bethlehem*. They then went directly to Egypt for a while, and attempted to move back to Judea (where Bethlehem is) after Herod died. It was only upon hearing that Archelaus was ruling in Judea that Joseph decided to relocate to Galilee (Mt.2:21-23).

Luke, however, affirms they *first lived in Galilee* (2:4) and only went to Bethlehem for a short while because of the census, then went immediately back after purification rites in the temple at Jerusalem. To think that you would write a history of someone's birth and just leave out having to flee for

---

[20] The city of Nazareth (in the region of Galilee) is approximately 70 miles north of Bethlehem (in the region of Judea), roughly the distance between Philadelphia and New York City.

your life to another country constitutes a shockingly poor biography. All of this makes sense when we realize that the gospel writers were composing these texts several decades later, and almost certainly were not eye witnesses of any of the events narrated. They just recorded what had been passed down to them by word of mouth or through other written sources.

4] What did Jesus do after his baptism?
Mt.4:1,2; Mk.1:12,13 Jesus went immediately into the desert for 40 days after baptism, to be tempted by the Devil.
Jn.2:1 Three days after his baptism, he was in a wedding at Cana. The temptation is not even mentioned at all in the gospel of John.

This is another case where the argument of omission does not hold water. Even Jesus could not be in the desert and at a wedding in Cana at the same time.

5] Is it alright to call people "fools"?
Mt.5:22 Jesus said to not call someone a "fool," and those who do are in danger of hell.
Mt.23:17 Jesus called the Pharisees "fools."

The Greek word for "fool" is identical in both texts. Not only is this a bad example on Jesus' part, it is ridiculous to think he would do something that he previously said would put us in danger of going to hell.

6] Did the centurion himself go to Jesus to request healing for his servant?
Mt.8:5,6 The centurion went himself to Jesus.
Lk.7:3,4 The centurion did *not* go himself but sent messengers to talk to Jesus.

This is another case that represents more than mere difference of viewpoint. Someone cannot both go and not go somewhere.

7] Where did Jesus heal the demoniac(s)?
Mt.8:28,29   Jesus healed the demoniacs in the region of the Gadarenes.
Mk.5:1; Lk.8:26 Jesus healed the demoniac in the region of the Gerasenes.

The numerous textual variants in the Greek manuscripts for these passages strongly suggest that they are referring to the same region and not two different places. This makes sense when we realize the copyists and possibly the writers themselves were most likely not familiar with Palestine geography.

8] How many demoniacs were there at the region of the Gadarenes/Gerasenes?
Mt.8:28,29 There were two demoniacs.
Mk.5:1-17; Lk.8:26-37 There was one demoniac.

A common defense for contradictions of this class is to argue that Mark and Luke only mention one when there were really two. But why would any credible historian write a narration about one man if he or she knew there were two involved? That would constitute very poor testimony, especially if the purpose in writing is to portray Christ as the Messiah. If two guys were seen saving someone from drowning, who would later describe them as "one man"? If Yahweh oversaw all of this process, it would have been very easily solved by just inspiring them to both put "two."

9] Did Jesus come to bring peace on earth?

Mt.10:34 "Do not think that I have come to bring peace to earth. *I did not come to bring peace* but a sword, to set a man against his father..."
Lk.2:14 At the birth of Jesus, the angels announced "peace on earth and goodwill toward men."
Jn.14:27 "Peace I leave with you, my peace I give unto you."
Acts 10:36 "Preaching peace through Jesus Christ..."

The Greek word for "peace" is identical in all these passages.

10] How many blind men did Jesus heal at Jericho?
Mt.20:29-30 Jesus healed two blind men at Jericho.
Mk.10:46; Lk.18:35-43 Jesus healed one blind man at Jericho.

This is not a case of two separate instances since all three passages show the same exchange between Jesus and the blind man/men. It is obviously referring to the same event. Also, notice that both here and in #8 above, Matthews affirms there were two when the other gospels say only one. There is a pattern of exaggeration throughout the gospel of Matthew that will be taken up later in section 2.3.

11] When exactly did Jesus heal the blind man/men at Jericho?
Mt.20:29-21:1; Mk.10:46-11:1 Jesus healed him/them upon *leaving* Jericho. He then went to Bethpage.
Lk.18:35-19:1 Jesus healed one blind man *on his way* to Jericho. He then entered Jericho to minister there.

I once heard a pastor (perhaps only jokingly) defend this by proposing Jericho was so small that entering and leaving were the same thing. Yet that still would not explain the subsequent verses that assert he went either to Bethpage or into Jericho.

12] Was Jesus' testimony about himself valid?
Jn.5:31 Jesus said that if he testified about himself, it was *not* valid.
Jn.8:14 Jesus said that if he testified about himself, it was valid.

Amazingly, the same Greek words appear for these two verses, with no textual variants in the manuscripts we possess. This is a clear type A contradiction, with a simple negation in one of the almost verbatim phrases. You could not be more contradictory if you tried.

13] Did Jesus come to judge the world?
Jn.9:39 "I have come to judge the world."
Jn.12:47 "I have *not* come to judge the world."

Just like above, the same Greek words are used for the entire sentence and there are no textual variants in the manuscripts we possess. This is another strong type A contradiction.

14] Did losing "one of those given him" fulfill Scripture?
Jn.17:12 Jesus lost *only one* of "those given him," in order to fulfill Scripture.
Jn.18:9 Jesus lost *none* of "those given him," in order to fulfill Scripture.

The Greek in both these phrases is virtually identical, including the word translated "lost." How can losing one and not losing one both fulfill Scripture?

15] Did Jesus ride one animal or two animals into Jerusalem?

Mt.21:2-7 The disciples went and untied two animals and brought them to Jesus. He then rode into Jerusalem on *two* animals, a colt and an adult donkey.
Mk.11:2-7 The disciples went and untied one animal and brought it to Jesus. He then rode into Jerusalem on *one* animal, a colt.

Some maintain that he sat on one while the other followed along, but neither gospel suggests that. The writer of Matthew specifically states Jesus sat on *them*, plural, and Mark never so much as mentions another animal in the entire narrative. This is no surprise with Matthew, who obviously says this in order to more accurately fulfill the Zechariah 9:9 "prophecy."[21] However, the Zechariah passage represents poetic alliteration and does not refer to two separate animals.[22]

16] What day was Jesus crucified?

Mk.14:12; Mk.15:1; Mk.15:25 Jesus was crucified the *second* day of the feast of Unleavened Bread (15ᵗʰ day of Nisan).

---

[21] "See, your king comes to you, righteous and victorious, lowly and riding on a donkey, on a colt, the foal of a donkey." (New International Version)
[22] See section 3.1 for other instances of forced prophecy fulfillment.

Jn.13:1; Jn.18:28; Jn.19:14   Jesus was crucified the *first* day of the feast of Unleavened Bread, "when they sacrifice the Passover lamb" (14th day of Nisan).

Dates in antiquity are always confusing, but scholars such as Bart Ehrman (2009:23-29) claim this is a legitimate contradiction.

17] What time of the day was Jesus crucified?
Mk.15:25 Jesus was crucified at the third hour.
Jn.19:13,14 Jesus was crucified after the sixth hour, since he was still before Pilate at "about the sixth hour."

Some have argued that Mark used a different time system than John. While this is theoretically possible, there is no clear evidence to suggest it. What we do know is several early copyists recognized a problem here and changed John 19:14 to say "about the third hour" in order to harmonize with Mark (Metzger 2005a:216). Such action certainly suggests a genuine contradiction.

18] Did both thieves mock Jesus on the cross?
Mt.27:44; Mk.15:32 Both of the thieves mocked Jesus.
Lk.23:39-40 Only one of the thieves mocked Jesus; the other defended him.

A common defense is that both thieves initially mocked Christ but one then changed his mind, yet this is pure speculation. None of the gospels suggests there was any change in one thief.

19] What did the Roman soldier say about Jesus?

Mk.15:39 The soldier said "truly this man was a son of God."
Lk.23:47 The soldier said "truly this man was righteous."

Although related, these statements are nonetheless distinct. Since Mark was written first[23] and it is possible Luke had access to it when composing his gospel, it is not clear why Luke would use a different phrase here.

20] Who went to Jesus' tomb after his death?
Mt.28:1 Mary Magdalene and another Mary went to the tomb.
Mk.16:1 Mary Magdalene, another Mary, and Salome went to the tomb.
Lk.24:1 Mary Magdalene, another Mary, Joanna, and "other women" went to the tomb.
Jn.20:1 Mary Magdalene went to the tomb.

Mary Magdalene is the only one common to all. Some have argued that even though John mentions just one woman, he uses a plural verb "*we* do not know" in 20:2, implying there were other people there. It is true the Greek verb is plural in that verse, but the rest of the passage is singular and when Mary Magdalene repeats herself in John 20:13 she says "*I* do not know."

---

[23] The general consensus among both liberal and conservative NT scholars in that Mark was the earliest gospel written, followed by Matthew, Luke, then John. The dates vary, but most estimate the composition of Mark at around 65-70 CE, Matthew and Luke 70-90 CE, and John 90 CE or later.

This is erratic and unconvincing testimony at best. What kind of historian would record only Mary Magdalene at the tomb if it was known that she went with at least five other women (the other Mary, Joanna, Salome, plus at least two more)? And why not be consistent with the verbs?

21] When did Mary Magdalene (with or without others) go to Jesus' tomb?

Mk.16:2 Mary Magdalene and another Mary went after the sun had risen.

Jn.20:1 Mary Magdalene went when it was still dark.

Mark 16:2 in Greek literally reads "having risen the sun" (an aorist participial phrase), and John 20:1 reads "early, while still dark." Solid evidence that this is a contradiction is seen in the fact that some manuscripts have this phrase in Mark either deleted entirely or changed to say "while the sun was rising." It is obvious that some scribes noticed a problem here and attempted to solve it by tampering with the text (Aland et al 2000:189).[24]

22] Was the rock rolled away when Mary Magdalene (and others) arrived? Were there guards there?

Mt.28:2 The women went to the tomb, then the rock was rolled away after an angel descended with a violent earthquake, while the guards looked on.

Mk.16:4; Lk.24:2; Jn.20:1 The rock was already rolled away and no guards are mentioned.

Mark 16:3 even affirms that while the women walked they were wondering who would move the

---

[24] See section 3.3 for further details.

stone away, but then they saw it was already done. No guards are mentioned at all in any gospel except Matthew.

23] Who was at the tomb when Mary Magdalene (and others) arrived?
Mt.28:2 One angel was at the tomb.
Mk.16:5 One young man was at the tomb.
Lk.24:4 Two men were at the tomb.
Jn.20:11,12 Two angels were at the tomb.

Notice that all four gospels conflict here. Some have insisted that "man" and "angel" can just be two ways of describing the same thing, since angels in the Bible typically take on human form. This is certainly true, but Greek had a word for "angel," another for "young man," and another for "man," so there is no reason as to why they could not just all use the same one. Furthermore, it still does not account for the discrepancy of number.

In order for all these to harmonize, conservatives must propose that there were really two angels at the tomb, yet only one out of four gospels actually says that. If Mark knew there were two angels, what would possibly motivate him to write "one young man" was there?

24] Where exactly were the angels/men in relation to the tomb?
Mt.28:2 The one angel came and sat on top of the rock, *outside* the tomb.
Mk.16:5 The young man was *already* sitting *inside* the tomb.
Lk.24:4 The two men *suddenly appeared* after the women went *inside* the tomb.

Jn.20:11,12 The two angels were *already inside* the tomb when Mary Magdalene looked.

This is one of the clearest and most irrefutable contradictions in relation to the resurrection. Each writer paints such a different picture, and I have yet to hear any plausible explanation for such disparity.

25] What was said to Mary Magdalene (and others) at the tomb?
Mt.28:7; Mk.16:7 "Jesus goes before you to Galilee. There you will see him."
Lk.24:6 "Remember what Jesus said while in Galilee."
Jn.20:17 "Go tell the disciples that I am returning to my father."

In Luke and John, no one said to go to Galilee at all.

26] What happened when Mary Magdalene (and others) left the tomb?
Mt.28:8 They ran to tell the disciples, then Jesus saw them on the way.
Mk.16:8 They ran in fear and did not say anything. There is no mention of seeing Jesus.[25]
Lk.24:8-11 The women went and told the disciples. There is no mention of seeing Jesus.
Jn.20:2 Mary Magdalene alone left running to tell the disciples, then came back with Peter and another disciple. Jesus then appeared to Mary Magdalene.

---

[25] Jesus appeared to the disciples in Mark 16:9-20, but virtually every scholar agrees these verses are a later interpolation as a way to smooth out the abruptness of Mark's original ending. See section 3.3 for more details.

27] What did the disciples do after the resurrection?

Mt.28:16 The disciples *went to Galilee* and saw Jesus. There is no mention of anything in Jerusalem.

Lk.24:13,33-36 That same day Jesus appeared to them and told them to *stay in Jerusalem*, which they did. They later went to Bethany, right outside of Jerusalem, where Jesus ascended to heaven.

Jn.20:19; Jn.21:1 The disciples *stayed in Jerusalem* in hiding for fear of the Jews and Jesus appeared to them "the same day" of his resurrection. Jesus appeared in Galilee over a week later.

This is quite clear and irrefutable. Galilee is 70 miles north of Jerusalem and would take days to walk there and at least one entire day to arrive on horse.

28] Where and to whom did Jesus appear after leaving the tomb?

Mt.28:17,18 Jesus appeared to his disciples in Galilee.

Mk.16 Mark registers no account of Jesus appearing at all.

Lk.24:15,36 Jesus appeared to two men walking to Emmaus (a town near Jerusalem), then to the disciples in Jerusalem.

Jn.20:19,26; Jn.21:1,14 Jesus appeared to the disciples on at least three separate occasions, at least a week apart, in Jerusalem and later on the shore of Lake Tiberias (the Sea of Galilee).

I Cor.15:3-8 Jesus appeared to Peter, then the disciples, then to 500 people at once, then to James, then to Paul.

Note that *not a single witness of these five is in complete agreement with the others*. It is also striking that only Paul, the earliest NT writer, references the 500 people who supposedly saw Jesus at once. That would have been remarkable evidence if true, yet no gospel writer even mentions it.

29] For how long did Jesus make appearances after the resurrection?

Lk.24:13,36,50-52   Jesus appeared only *one* day. Having seen his disciples "that same day" he was resurrected, he then went to Bethany (right outside of Jerusalem) and ascended to heaven. This is the very end of Luke's gospel.

Jn.20:19,26; Jn.21:14 Jesus appeared throughout at least *eight* days, once the day of the resurrection, then again up north at Lake Tiberias. There is no ascension mentioned at all.

Acts 1:3   Jesus appeared throughout 40 days.

Some argue that Jesus could have been coming and going but the gospel of Luke does not suggest this at all. It ends with the ascension, which is strongly suggested by the context to be the very same day he resurrected. This confusion becomes even more surprising given the fact that the gospel of Luke and Acts were most likely written by the same author.

CHAPTER TWO: ABSURDITIES IN THE BIBLE

Merriam-Webster defines the word *absurd* as something "unreasonable, unsound, incongruous, extremely silly, or ridiculous; having no rational or orderly relationship to human life." Although such a classification is inevitably subjective to a certain degree, I think most readers will agree the following items can indeed be categorized as such.

2.1 MORAL ABSURDITIES

Even if there were viable explanations for all of the contradictions mentioned above, Christians have all their work ahead of them in rationalizing the outrageous morality presented in Scripture. Whether they admit it or not, the fact of the matter is their holy book condones polygamy, slavery, genocide, misogyny, and racism. These alone are reason enough to reject the Bible as "holy."

It cannot be legitimately argued that such teachings were inspired by a loving, merciful, and immutable god. The only way any of it makes sense is if we realize the Bible was written in a very different time by people with a very different view of social justice. Religion is human and has changed just like everything else. At that stage in history, numerous cultures had no qualms about brutally slaughtering foreign people groups and treating women like cattle. Since so many lived that way, it was not a big deal to them. They did what they could to survive in an unstable and underdeveloped world. Yet it therefore cannot be said that Scripture is the source of our morality. In fact, it is only in very recent years that society has woken up to the injustice of many of these issues.[26]

Among other things, the following verses will demonstrate that Yahweh and ancient Israel were virtually indistinguishable from Allah and militant Islam today:

> Brutal punishment for breaking religious laws? Yes.
> Killing other people, including women and children, because of their beliefs? Yes.
> Stealing land, belongings, and women of others? Yes.
> Polygamy and oppression of women? Yes.
> Recalcitrant insistence on their variety of monotheism? Yes.

1] Yahweh drowned every child on the planet in the flood. Gen.7:22,23.

Pretty much everything about the flood story is illogical. An all-knowing and all-powerful god created man, and when they did not turn out as planned (surprisingly?), the best way to deal with it was to drown everyone including animals and plants and "start over" with the same beings, who very quickly went back to doing all they did before. The whole trouble of building an ark and gathering

---

[26] In America, a country supposedly founded on Christian principles and at the vanguard of social liberty, a mere century has passed since women have had the right to vote, and only half that time has interracial marriage been legal in all 50 states.

animals could have been avoided by just giving the perpetrators a heart attack or a plague or something similar.

Why kill everything including children, animals, and plants? Starting over with Noah was supposed to remedy the situation? Was there really no hope for any human being other than Noah and his family? They were all, to the very last toddler, hopelessly evil?

Another important consideration is the fact that there most certainly were numerous pregnant women at that time whose unborn children were killed in the flood. It goes without saying that such an occurrence is in direct opposition to the current "pro-life" message.

These moral and theological implications of the flood are of course totally separate from the scientific problems with the narrative, for which virtually every biological and geological evidence is against.

2] Lot was righteous? Gen.19; II Pet.2:7.

Lot is said to have offered his virgin daughters to be raped by an unruly mob, then later got so drunk that he impregnated both of them. Nevertheless, the author of II Peter asserts that Lot was a righteous man and suffered while living among the perverse Sodomites.

3] Human sacrifice was acceptable if done for Yahweh. Gen.22; Lev.27:28,29; Jud.11:31-39.

Abraham was *commanded* to sacrifice Isaac, and Jephthah sacrificed his daughter in order to fulfill a vow. Although Isaac did not actually die, Jephthah did kill his daughter. Nowhere are they even suggested to have done wrong. In fact, they are both *praised* in

Hebrews 11 as people who "did justly." Scripture therefore presents stabbing a child to death as a logical way to prove dedication to a loving god.

At other times, Israelites could consecrate animals or persons to Yahweh and sacrifice them as a dedication offering. Leviticus 27 shows the prices for such circumstances when people would make a vow and then "redeem" it by paying the priests. Yet sometimes that was not possible and the victim was sacrificed. Surprisingly, Moody even confirms this was the case. Child sacrifice is condemned multiple times in the OT, yet every time *it is because it was done for other gods*, like Molech or Baal (Dt.12:31; Lev.20:1,2; II Kg.16:3; II Kg.17:17; Jer.7:31; Ez.16:20-21).

4] Slavery was bad only if it was Israel who was enslaved.   Ex.3:16,17;   Ex.12:44;   Ex.21:4; Lev.25; Dt.21; Dt.24:7.

Yahweh allegedly pitied Israel's mistreatment as slaves, yet later in the same book allowed them to have slaves and beat them with rods (see #12 of this section). Exodus 21:4 also established that the slave's wife and children were the owner's property for life.

Most conservatives will argue that the ancient system really was not as cruel as the more recent British and American slave trade in West Africa, and point out that Jews themselves could be sold temporarily as indentured servants in order to pay off a debt. The latter is certainly true, but the former is unjustifiable according to Scripture. Deuteronomy 24:7 even decrees that anyone who kidnaps an Israelite and treats him like a slave will be killed, because it is "evil."

OT slavery was fundamentally the same as modern slavery:

A] Most slaves were non-Jewish victims of war, including women and children. It had nothing to do with paying off debt.
B] They were forced to do physical labor projects in Israel. *Slaves were even used to build Solomon's temple* (I Kg.9:15-21).
C] They had no hope of escaping their situation. They and their families were considered property of the Jews and could even be passed on as part of an inheritance.

5] Yahweh himself makes people blind and deaf. Ex.4:11.

Compare Leviticus 21:18-20 in which the blind, deaf, or crippled were prohibited from presenting offerings as priests in the temple.

6] Yahweh killed all Egyptian firstborns because Pharaoh would not release Israel. Ex.4:22-23; Ex.12.

Notice that even children of prisoners were killed (12:29), who could have had no part in Pharaoh's decisions. To Yahweh, it was worse to enslave an Israelite than to kill an Egyptian.

7] Yahweh tried to kill Moses for not circumcising his son. Ex.4:24.

This came right after choosing him to deliver his people. Failing to circumcise his son was apparently more egregious than murdering an Egyptian, which Moses had just done (Ex.2:11,12).

Circumcision itself never made any sense to me, even as a believer. Yahweh "intelligently designed" the human body with a foreskin and then subsequently told them to cut it off as a sign that they were chosen? Furthermore, it reiterated a sexist separation in Israel, since this choosing obviously only applied to men. Similar things can be said in regard to much of the OT laws.

8] Yahweh hardened Pharaoh's heart, then punished all of Egypt for it. Ex.10:1,2; Ex.12.

As mentioned above, all Egyptian firstborns were killed due to Pharaoh's unwillingness to release the Jews from bondage. Nine other plagues were sent as well which affected everyone in that region. Yahweh himself admitted he was responsible and did it so that Israel would have stories to tell their grandchildren (12:25-27).

9] Yahweh is portrayed as just, yet regularly punished the innocent for other people's sins.

In addition to #6 and #8 above, there are several instances of this:

A] An illegitimate child could not enter Yahweh's assembly up to the tenth generation. Dt.23:2.

B] Achan's entire family, including sons and daughters, were stoned to death because he took spoils from Jericho. Jos.8:24,25.

C] The Israelites were punished with three years of famine for what Saul did to the Gibeonites. II Sam.21:1.

D] 70 thousand people (the size of a medium city by today's standards) died because of David's census. II Sam.24:1-15.

E] Job's ten children were killed as part of a bet with Satan. Job 1.

F] Every person alive was born sinful because Adam ate from the tree in the garden. Rom.5:12.

**10] Polygamy was acceptable (for men only).
Ex.21:10; Dt.21:15.**

In addition to the above verses, it is important to note Jacob himself had children with four different women. Other revered leaders who were said to have Yahweh's favor had multiple wives and/or concubines, such as Abraham (at least two concubines in Genesis 25:5), David (at least nine wives), and Abijah (fourteen wives in II Chronicles 13:21). Nowhere are these men criticized for this. Solomon, with his 700 wives and 300 concubines, was condemned only because they were foreign and "perverted his heart" away from Yahweh, causing him to worship other gods, not because of polygamy in itself (I Kg.11:1-8). The modern conservatives who use Scripture to support a "traditional marriage" (one man + one woman) are gravely mistaken. *Traditional biblical marriage was polygamy.*

11] Israel was to execute those who cursed their parents or were obstinate. Ex.21:17; Dt.21:18-21.

Law and order are necessary for any functional society, but the Pentateuch is full of extremely over-the-top punishments. As this and other citations show, many relatively petty crimes were punishable by death. Some apologists defend these actions by declaring them to be the only viable option for a newly formed people group who were wandering the desert. Nevertheless, these same chapters also list multiple crimes that were punishable only by a monetary fine, so we know there were other options and such brutality was not necessary.

12] Beating female slaves with rods was acceptable. Ex.21:20,21.

These verses state that "when a man strikes his slave, male or female, with a rod...and the slave survives in a day or two, he is not to be avenged (the owner does not have to pay or be killed), for *the slave is his property.*" This goes blatantly against McDowell's (2013:96) claim that "slaves were treated more as employees by Israel and not as property to be mistreated."

Also, the famous "eye for eye, tooth for tooth" of Exodus 21:26,27 did not apply to slaves. If an owner hit his slave and knocked an eye out, the owner's eye would not be knocked out; he only had to release the slave. It is interesting to note that Exodus 21 comes immediately after the first Ten Commandments, which are supposedly the foundation of Western morality.

13] Adultery was a capital crime. Lev.20:10.
"If a man commits adultery with another man's wife, both the adulterer and the adulteress are to be put to death." There are no doubt many believers, pastors included, who are relieved that this mandate is no longer obeyed.

14] Yahweh commanded Israel to execute homosexuals. Lev.20:13.
"If a man has sexual relations with a man as one does with a woman, both of them have done what is detestable. They are to be put to death; their blood will be on their own heads."

15] Israel was to burn certain prostitutes alive. Lev.21:9.
This particular punishment only applied to daughters of priests, but it is shameful that anyone would be subject to such a barbaric execution. Not

only were they to kill the women for doing something that could only exist if there were male customers, they were to do it in an unnecessarily torturous way.

16] Israel was to stone people for taking Yahweh's name in vain. Lev.24:10-16.

Blasphemy is a capital offense in the Bible, yet modern Christianity criticizes militant Islam for doing such things.

17] Israel attempted forced miscarriages and sterilization (i.e. abortion). Num.5:11-31.

When a woman was accused of adultery, they were to take her before the priest and force her to drink what would supposedly produce miscarriage and sterilization if pregnant.

Even Moody admits this and justifies it by proposing that Israel could not allow illegitimate children to become a weight for the people! This is therefore *a primitive attempt at abortion mandated in Scripture*, and there is no way around it. Regardless of the efficacy of the practice, it nonetheless is very absurd from a theological and moral standpoint. I am certain many staunch "pro-life" believers are not even aware of these verses.

18] Israel stoned a man for gathering wood on Sabbath. Num.15:32-36.

This is yet another case of brutal execution for a petty crime.

19] Yahweh ordered revenge that was not really revenge. Num.31.

Yahweh ordered Moses to exterminate the Midianites as punishment for having fornicated with the Israelite men, who had chosen to have sex with prostitutes and worship Baal out of their own free will. Besides the issue of Yahweh ordering revenge under any circumstance, the Midianites really did nothing to deserve such a massacre. Notice Israel even killed all the Midianite *children* (31:17), but kept the virgin women as spoils of war (one can only imagine what for), counting them along with the cattle (31:32-35).

20] Yahweh hardened more hearts and gave no mercy. Dt.2:30-35; Jos.11:20.

Yahweh hardened the heart of the Canaanite king Sihon so he would make war with the Jewish people. He later did so with other inhabitants of that region "so that they should come against Israel in battle, in order that they should be devoted to destruction and should receive no mercy but be destroyed."

21] Israel systematically slaughtered women and children then took their belongings. Dt.2:34,35; Dt.3:4-7; I Sam.15:3.

Scripture maintains that Israel conquered over 60 cities, "killing all their men, women and children," but kept the animals and things of value. Later on, Yahweh specifically ordered the massacre of all Amalekite children and infants.

As much as I have tried to listen to conservative explanations, I still find no sensible justification for this. We have to face the facts that, according to the text, the Israelites invaded Canaan, murdering and stealing everything they could, no different from Assyria, Babylon, Greece, Rome, or the Vandals.

Even if the Canaanites were irreparably evil, a common argument among evangelicals, that would have no relation whatsoever to the Jewish people.

Yahweh could have just extinguished them himself, as he is said to have done in the universal flood and with Sodom and Gomorrah. He would not have needed human swords in Canaan. If they sinned against him, *he* should have done the punishing without bringing Israel into it.

If I proposed that the German and Polish Jews, even the children, were so evil that Hitler was warranted in murdering six million of them, people would justifiably think I was a complete madman, yet that is exactly the defense most conservatives give concerning Israel's holy war.

What was Yahweh teaching by having them slaughter entire people groups, including women and children, and then take their possessions? That was how Yahweh was going to spread his message of salvation, peace, and love? Surely there was a better way.

And how were the Canaanites so irreparably evil? The answer most Christians offer tends to include three main characteristics: child sacrifice, violence, and sexual immorality.[27] As has already been shown, citing child sacrifice as "wicked" is hypocritical to say the least, since Yahweh commanded it with Abraham, and condoned it with Jephthah and others.

Claiming the Canaanites were wicked because of their violence is even more nonsensical. Yahweh used extreme violence, even against children, as punishment for being violent? Also, if this is true then modern secular society is more merciful than Yahweh, since most countries just lock up violent offenders without executing them.

---

[27] Paul Copan's 2011 publication *Is God a Moral Monster?* is a perfect example of such a defense of the extermination of the Canaanites.

In regard to sexuality, if their crimes entailed relations outside of heterosexual marriage, then there has not been a single people group in recorded history innocent of such charges. If Yahweh killed the Canaanites, he would be equally justified in doing so with Americans. We fornicate, commit adultery, look at pornography, and rape to the same degree as everyone else (if not higher). Why are we still alive, then?

Every evangelical argument I have heard about the OT genocide is extremely unconvincing. They have to twist and stretch the text so much that it makes them look foolish. It is disappointing anyone can be so intellectually dishonest.

22] Israel was ordered to stone apostates. Dt.13:6-10.

Those who suggested worshiping other gods were to be executed, even their own family members. Those closest to the victim were to be the ones who threw the first stone, and were not to show compassion. How can such a system generate authentic belief? *If there is no freedom to dissent, there is no freedom at all.*

23] It was alright to steal foreign women and have sex with them. Dt.21:10-21.

Yahweh allowed the Jews to take attractive female prisoners of war as wives by force, then let them go if they were not "pleasing" to them. The Canaanites were so wicked they had to be annihilated, but Israel could have children with the virgins? Would not the offspring have been half wicked?

24] Israel was to stone women who were not virgins at marriage, yet rape was only mildly punished. Dt.22:20-29.

A girl found to have had sex before marriage was to be executed, yet if a man raped someone, he only had to pay 50 shekels of silver then marry the victim. This is virtually identical to modern militant Islam in its treatment of women. Imagine being the woman who was forced to marry her rapist.

25] Yahweh punished illegitimate children and children of other ethnicities. Dt.23:2,3.

An illegitimate child could not enter Yahweh's assembly, neither could his children up to ten generations. A Moabite or Ammonite child could not enter either, up to ten generations, for the way their ancestors treated Israel when they were fleeing Egypt.

26] Yahweh ordered Israel to cut off a woman's hand it she touched a man's genitals during a fight. Dt.25:11-12.

The verses stress that they should "not have compassion" on her when dealing out the punishment.

27] Yahweh wanted to "teach Israel how to war." Jud.2:23-3:3.

Yahweh himself allegedly left some nations unconquered only so the remaining generations of Israel would have someone to practice their fighting skills with.

It seems evident the writers needed to explain why all the Canaanites were not eliminated, so they came up with this reason. This is another case of the failed logic some religious people have in regard to events in their lives. When things go well, it is because their god is with them, yet when things turn out poorly, it is because they are being tested, punished for sin, or prepared for a future challenge. The same was true for the ancients. If they won a battle, it was credited to their god, but if they lost, it was because of their own failures. It was impossible for Yahweh to lose in such a system, and it works the same if you substitute in Allah or Zeus.

Look at the battles with Ai, for example, in Joshua 8:1-29. Israel lost the first time because they overconfidently sent only a few thousand men, but won the second time because they had a better strategy with more people. There was nothing miraculous involved; it was simple warfare. Yet Achan's entire family was executed for allegedly causing the loss by their sin.

28] Yahweh gave David's concubines to Absalom to be raped in public. II Sam.12:11.

Yahweh had the concubines raped by Absalom as punishment for David's adultery. The text clearly states he himself was behind it.

29] Yahweh killed a baby as further punishment for David's adultery. II Sam.12:14.

The baby killed was the one Bathsheba conceived by David. This is another difficult case for the modern "pro-life" crowd to explain.

30] Yahweh sent lies and actively deceived people.

A] Yahweh held a conference in heaven and asked who would get Ahab to attack the city of Ramoth so he would die in battle (although an omnipotent god could have just killed Ahab himself). He then got an angel volunteer to go and lie to them so Ahab would attack. Yahweh approved of the lying angel and sent him. I Kg.22:19-23.

B] Yahweh himself insisted he enticed and deceived certain prophets then punished them for it. Ez.14:9.

C] Yahweh actively will deceive people by sending a delusion. II Thess.2:11.

31] Yahweh sent bears to maul 42 youths who mocked Elisha's baldness. II Kg.2:23-25.

There has understandably been much debate in regard to the interpretation of this short yet extremely bizarre incident, with the main controversy revolving around who the victims were and what their age was. Part of the problem stems from the fact that the Hebrew word translated "boys" in verse 23 is also used in other parts of the OT to mean "servant." Therefore, some have argued that it should be translated "servants" instead, implying that they were killed due to their affiliation with other gods. However, even if that were true, the Hebrew also includes the adjective "little" or "small" in verse 23, so it is clear they were not adults, as is supported in the fact that every mainstream translation uses some form of "boy" rather than "servant" in II Kings 2:23.

Nevertheless, due to the undefined age of the victims, other evangelicals have offered the explanation that it really was a band of dangerous teenagers threatening Elisha with bodily harm (Strobel 2000:122-125). As is usually the case, the problem is the text simply does not say that. It affirms they were youths who made fun of his baldness, without implying they were armed and dangerous at all, unless being numerous in itself is a threat.

Even if they were aggressive, they did not need to be killed in such a brutal way. Yahweh could have put a protective wall around Elisha or something similar. The only solution was to have bears rip them to shreds? This passage is irrational even if we interpret the victims as teenage servants, much more if they were children, as the majority of Hebrew scholars have translated it.

32] Yahweh inspired the psalmist to write of revolting violence. Ps.137:7,8.

"Lord remember the Edomites...blessed are those who make you pay for what you did to us, blessed are those who take your little ones and bash them against the rock."

Although not a mandate from Yahweh, this psalm of bloodthirsty revenge is part of the accepted canon and is therefore alleged to be inspired by him. It is perhaps the most sickening picture of violence in the entire Bible. How this is supposed to speak to us is a mystery.

33] Yahweh hated Esau, and hardened certain people's hearts. Rom.9:11-18.

Paul maintains that Yahweh hated Esau for no reason, even before he was born, and that he hardens people's hearts when they have done nothing to deserve it nor can do anything to change it. Is there a greater injustice than this? A god who does such things cannot be considered good and worthy of praise.

As mentioned in the contradiction section regarding this verse, the Greek word here is the most common word for "hate" and is the same as in I John 3:15, which reads that "whoever hates his brother is a murderer, and you know that no murderer has eternal life abiding in him." Yahweh is thus doing something the rest of the NT portrays as characterizing unbelievers.

34] Yahweh wants women to be silent in church and call their husbands "Lord." I Cor.14:34,35; I Pt.3:6.

All monotheisms have viewed women as less important, less intelligent, and less capable of making decisions. Notice only in recent history have women begun to hold positions of authority in American politics and religion, due mostly to *secular* pressure for equal rights.

35] Yahweh did not like Cretans. Tit.1:12.

"Cretans are always liars, evil brutes, and lazy gluttons. This word is true." Besides being an obvious exaggeration, it is openly prejudice as well. Evidently the author did not expect any Cretans to read his epistle. Put it in modern terms and think about the equivalent statement: "Americans are all lazy, dishonest gluttons." Not a single Cretan was honest and hardworking? Every single one lied at every opportunity? Such allegations are simply impossible to believe. Their society would have been entirely unsustainable if that were the case.

36] Israelites are commanded to be racist throughout the Bible.

There is no hope for anyone who is not Jewish until after Jesus is said to have resurrected. The idea of ethnic cleansing and purity is pervasive, even in the gospels. Jesus himself told a Gentile woman that he was sent to the Jews, not to Gentiles, and then called her a "dog" (Mt.15:24-26). Several times the Israelites are strongly condemned for marrying into other people groups and are even forced to abandon their foreign wives and children (Ezra 10:9-44; Neh.13:23-27). This is stridently opposed to the idea of divine love for all, neither Jew nor Greek, presented in Paul's letters. It teaches open racism and ethnic superiority, which is sadly ironic given the horrific persecution the Jewish people themselves have suffered throughout history.

2.2 THEOLOGICAL ABSURDITIES

1] Yahweh regretted making man and was "sorry in his heart." Gen.6:6.

It is completely illogical that an omniscient god with a perfect plan would regret anything. It was a surprise that man turned out exactly how he was created to turn out? Even if it only means Yahweh was saddened, as some claim, it still does not make sense given that he would have known the outcome from the beginning.

2] Moses reasoned with Yahweh and convinced him to change his mind. Ex.32:9-14.

The god of Israel became angry and threatened to kill them all due to their obstinacy, so Moses pleaded with him to remember his promises and to consider what Egypt would think if they found out. Yahweh then relented and changed his mind.

3] Yahweh acted like an adolescent. Ex.32:34; Ex.33:2-5.

Yahweh told Moses to go on ahead to the Promised Land without him, and he would not accompany them because they were "a stubborn people" and he "might destroy [them] along the way."

4] Iron chariots were too much for Yahweh. Jud.1:19.

"Yahweh was with the Israelites but they could not drive out those who lived in the plain because they had chariots of iron." No part of this makes sense.

5] Moses reasoned with Yahweh and convinced him a second time. Num.14:10-23.

Angry with the Israelites' complaints about the desert, Yahweh declared to Moses that he would "strike them down with a plague and destroy them." Moses then reminded him he could not do that because the Egyptians would hear about it and tell everyone how he was not able to get his people to the Promised Land. Yahweh then rescinded and decided to just bar everyone over 20 years of age from entering the land.

6] Yahweh lost his temper and killed 14,700 people in the process. Num.16:41-50.

The people complained about Moses, so Yahweh threatened to kill all of them at once (again). Moses told Aaron to "quick, go get a censor and intercede for the people." Aaron did so, but only after Yahweh had already killed 14,700 people in a plague. His incense stopped the slaughter.

7] Yahweh sent an evil spirit to torment Saul who later tried to kill David. I Sam.16:14; I Sam.18:10.

Not only is there the issue of an evil spirit tormenting at Yahweh's bidding, but also that the same spirit later prompted Saul to try and kill David, the future anointed who would be one of the most important figures outside of Christ.

8] Yahweh created evil. Is.45:7.

"I make peace and create evil. I the Lord do all these things." The Hebrew word "create" here is the same as in Genesis 1:1, and "evil" is identical to that used in Genesis 3:5,22. Many translators unsurprisingly have chosen "calamity" over "evil" in an attempt to minimize the absurdity, but there is absolutely no linguistic reason to do this. "I, Yahweh, create evil" is a perfectly accurate translation and is exactly how the Septuagint reads as well. Even if it possibly could mean merely "calamity," that still presents a problem since Yahweh himself would be admitting responsibility for at least part of the bad that happens in the world.

9] There is a complete lack of teaching about heaven and hell in the OT.

Nowhere in the entire OT did Yahweh urge his people to do right for heavenly rewards or to avoid eternal punishment. Time and time again, he commanded them to obey so they would be blessed with abundant crops and large families, and threatened them with drought, disease, and captivity if they disobeyed (Deuteronomy 28 is a good example). Not only is this different from Jesus' teaching of "lay up your treasures in heaven," it is contradictory. Are we supposed to want earthly prosperity or not? Furthermore, if there is a heaven and hell, that would be the single most important bit of information humans could know. To think a loving god would simply not mention it is truly incredible.

10] There is no clear teaching of a Trinity in the OT.

This foundational belief of Christianity is nowhere to be found until the NT writings. Before that, the Messiah was never taught to be equal with Yahweh and the Holy Spirit was not mentioned at all. Some point to the plural in verses like Genesis 1:26 "let us make man in our image," but one of the Hebrew words for "god" is *Elohim*, which is grammatically plural. Others make the case that certain appearances of supernatural figures were the pre-incarnate Christ (as in Joshua 5:13-15), but nowhere does the text openly propose anything like that.

The OT teaches explicitly that Yahweh is one and never suggests three figures of a godhead (Dt.4:35; Dt.6:4; II Sam.22:32; I Kg.8:60). The Trinity appears to be a much later religious development due to the fact that most early Christians considered Jesus to be divine also.[28]

11] Nowhere in the OT are the Jewish people commanded or even encouraged to evangelize.

Most of the time, their dealings with neighboring people were conflictive, with war or prophetic threats. Besides the story of Jonah preaching to the Assyrians, Yahweh cared very little about Gentiles until after the first century CE, for even Jesus spent almost his entire ministry only with Jews. If everyone who did not believe in Yahweh was doomed for eternity (although that is not taught in the OT, as mentioned above), next to nothing was done to remedy the situation.

---

[28] In multiple publications, Bart Ehrman deals extensively with the development of the doctrine of the Trinity and other related teachings, most notably in *Lost Christianities* (2005).

12] Jesus said if two believers agree about anything they ask, the Father will do it for them. He later said "whatever you ask in prayer, if you have faith, you will receive it." Mt.18:19; Mt.21:22; Mk.11:24.

Neither of these can be literally true; they have been tested repeatedly and shown to fail. If they are not literally true, what is the point of the verses? To assure us that we will only sometimes receive what we ask? Such an affirmation would provide little comfort indeed.

13] Jesus spoke in parables to hide his message from the rest. Mk.4:11-12.

"To you [disciples] has been given the mystery of the kingdom of God, but to those outside everything is in parables, *so that seeing they may not perceive*...lest they turn and be forgiven."

14] Jesus cursed a fig tree. Mk.11:12-14,20-21.

Jesus cursed the tree for not bearing fruit out of season. If it was not the season, why would he get angry? He could have just performed a miracle and made it bear fruit anyway. This passage is completely illogical.

15] Satan has power to blind people from the gospel. II Cor.4:4.

"The god of this world has blinded the mind of the unbelievers, to keep them from seeing the light of the gospel..." It cannot be maintained that Yahweh is all-powerful and wants everyone to be saved, if Satan is able to keep that from happening. How can these unbelievers be justly condemned? One who is blinded by another cannot be at fault. It is equivalent to putting a blindfold on a child and then punishing him or her for walking into a wall.

16] The Bible includes extensive sections of insignificant information, yet fails to mention issues of vital importance.
Genesis contains genealogies of Esau, Ezra gives detailed accounts of the names and numbers of people returning from captivity, and Ezekiel spends several chapters giving dimensions for a temple that was never built. Yet the entire OT fails to even mention heaven or hell.

2.3 FACTUAL ABSURDITIES AND EXAGGERATIONS

I realize the Bible uses round numbers, metaphor, symbols, and similes. It does not always use them, however, and often is very literal and specific in its details, as Genesis 12, Numbers 3, and Ezra 2 illustrate. How do we know when the text is giving accurate historical information or simply embellishing to make a point? How do we know what really happened? Is it not possible that some events like David and Goliath, Daniel in the lions' den, and Jesus feeding 5,000 people could have been embellished as well? Where does the metaphor stop and the literal meaning begin? An honest look at many of the following verses will demonstrate that the Bible unmistakably makes false claims about history.

1] The creation account. Gen.1,2.
It is nearly impossible to believe in a 6,000-10,000 year old earth in light of modern science. The evidence on many levels has proven Genesis to be

simply wrong in regard to the time and manner of life's origins and to the development of animal species. So much data goes against it that even millions of Christians have recognized this and accepted evolution with its geological time frame, mostly by holding to a metaphorical interpretation of the creation account.

While this is at least more honest than clinging to a literal reading of Scripture, it does not seem the original writers meant it to be metaphor, and certainly throughout history that has not been the most common belief. Why would Yahweh give us Genesis 1 if the universe is really billions of years old and there were several pre-human species that lived and died on earth? Why not reveal what actually happened instead of telling us fables about gardens and talking snakes? I realize the Bible is not a science textbook, but it could have easily explained to us at least the basic tenets of biology without having to discover it all on our own many centuries later.

There are so many quality books written on this topic that I will not delve any further here but rather point the reader to any one of the relevant sources listed in the bibliography.

2] Adam lived 930 years, Methuselah 969 years, etc. Gen.5:5,27.

According to creationists, there was a canopy over the earth that enabled humans to live so long, and after the flood their lives began to shorten. Even if this were plausible (and it is not, given what we know about the earth), *after* the flood certain men also allegedly lived well over 100 (Moses 120 years, Joshua 110). We know for a fact that people in the ancient world lived much shorter lives, not longer. The average lifespan for a Roman is estimated to have been about 40-50 years, without taking into consideration the exceedingly high infant mortality rates. Even with all the modern medical treatments and nutrition we have today, the vast majority of people do not live 100 years. These exaggerated passages make perfect sense, however, when we consider that the Israelite worldview perceived long earthly life to be a blessing for having pleased Yahweh.

3] Celestial beings were attracted to humans and their sexual union produced "giants of renown." Gen.6:1-4.

Although the exact interpretation of this outrageous claim has been debated among scholars for centuries, it is a widespread belief that this passage literally refers to sexual reproduction between supernatural beings and female humans. Such is the opinion of Moody and other mainstream Protestant commentators.

4] There were 603,550 Israelite men over 20 years old who left Egypt during the Exodus. Ex.12:37; Ex.38:26.

This is hardly to be seen as a round number with symbolic meaning. It is a literal claim to a precise number at a specific place and time. Including women and children, that would have been a minimum of 1,200,000 people, and probably closer to two million. Given what we know about ancient populations, it is highly unlikely to be true. A group this size, even without accounting for livestock, would have formed a line dozens of miles long. It is simply too many people.

That many Israelites, with animals and belongings, wandering in Sinai for 40 years (if even possible given the terrain) would have left an enormous amount of artifacts, bones, and the like. Finkelstein and Silberman (2002) declare that repeated excavations have revealed nothing close to this, not even the slightest evidence that such a migration ever occurred, even around Kadesh-Barnea, where they supposedly camped for years.

5] Sprinkling blood of sacrificed birds purified a house of mold. Lev.14:33-53.

Yahweh showed the people how to "purify" a house infected by mold that he himself put there (14:34). After inspecting it and watching it for a period, they were to kill a bird and sprinkle the blood with water on the walls for it to be clean.

Such actions were nothing more than ancient mysticism which solved nothing, like a voodoo shaman blowing smoke and mumbling a few phrases over a sick child. Why would Yahweh not have actually given them some real medical advice, like details about germs and how they could be sterilized?

6] Samson killed 1,000 men in a single day with the jawbone of a donkey. Jud.15:15.

Even as a kid in Sunday school I always had trouble imagining such an event. One person could not do this even with a rifle and 10 hand grenades. Did they just line up and wait for Samson to come along one by one to hit them in the head with a jawbone? After 700 or so, no one simply decided to abandon the effort? If it was a miracle, then there was no need for a weapon at all. An all-powerful god could have just made them all drop dead on the spot.

7] There were 700 men who could sling a stone at a hair and not miss. Jud.20:16.

This can be nothing but exaggeration.

8] Joseb Basebeth killed 800 men in a single day with a spear. II Sam.23:8.
Like the Samson example above, how in the world would someone actually do this?

9] The Israelites killed 100,000 Syrians in one day. Later, the city wall collapsed and killed 27,000 more. I Kg.20:29-30.
Both these numbers are astoundingly high. The battle of Gettysburg, the bloodiest battle of the American Civil War, took place over three entire days and even then only about 50,000 people died *total on both sides*, with guns and cannons. One of the bloodiest days in modern history was the first day of the Somme offensive in World War I, and only about 60,000 British soldiers were killed. Also, how exactly does a wall fall on 27,000 people? Even if they lived in the wall, this is pretty hard to imagine.

10] Solomon sacrificed 22,000 oxen and 120,000 sheep in one week. II Chr.7:5.
With a total of 142,000 animals, they would constitute approximately 850 sacrifices per hour for seven days straight. It is hard to believe there would have been any animals left in all of Israel after this.

11] Abijah sent 400,000 men into battle against Jeroboam's 800,000 men. II Chr.13:3.
This is a total of 1,200,000 men, all of them Jews of fighting age. Modestly assuming one woman plus two other persons (either elderly or children) per man, that would put the Jewish population of the surrounding area at a minimum of 4.8 million people.
Although the numbers do not sound remarkable from a modern standpoint, they are very improbable. Modern estimates of large ancient cities

like Babylon and Nineveh are not even 500,000 total people, let alone men of fighting age. The city of Rome at its height probably only had about a million inhabitants. For this passage to be true, ancient Israel would have had at least *four* cities as big as ancient Rome, in an area about the size of the state of Massachusetts. Even in today's highly urbanized world, the total population of Israel is only about eight million, not even twice what the Bible claims is was over 2,500 years ago.

12] 500,000 Israelites died in a single battle with Judah. II Chr.13:17.
Some versions like the New International read "casualties" instead of "deaths," no doubt in an attempt to minimize the incredible nature of the claim. The majority have "deaths" or "killed," however. According to *Strong's Concordance*, the Hebrew word used here means "slain, killed, mortally wounded." Note also that these are only the northern tribes of Israel, not including Judah. And although the biblical text does not say how long the battle lasted, it is portrayed as a single event and not a drawn-out military campaign.

500,000 is more than were lost in any single battle of any war documented in modern history (with machine guns, bombs, grenades, etc.), and even exceeds the number of deaths that resulted from the *dropping of the atomic bombs on Nagasaki and Hiroshima*, from which about 250,000 died.

Certain confrontations such as the battle of Stalingrad had several hundred thousand total deaths, yet these were actually long military campaigns which lasted several weeks or even months. Even if II Chronicles 13 is not an exaggeration, the loss of so many men would effectively have wiped out any people group of that time. The following generation at best would have been only 50% Jewish due to necessary intermarrying with other ethnicities.

13] Matthew exaggerates Jesus' actions and teachings.

A] As noted in section 1.6, at least twice Matthew claims there were two people healed when Mark and Luke say only one. Since Mark was written first, Matthew is likely changing Mark's narrative to make it more impactful. Compare Matthew 8:28,29 and 20:29,30 with Mark 5:1, 10:46 and Luke 8:26, 18:35.

B] Matthew is the only one who maintains Jesus told the twelve disciples to "raise the dead" when he sent them out to minister two by two (10:8). In Mark and Luke, he only commanded them to heal the sick and cast out demons.

C] Matthew is the only one who says Peter also walked on water by Jesus' command and that the disciples then worshiped Jesus declaring him to be the "son of God." Compare Matthew 14:22-33, Mark 6:45-52, and John 6:16-21.

14] Matthew makes extraordinary additions to the resurrection narrative. Mt.27:51-28:15.

He asserts there was an earthquake, other saints were resurrected, and the Roman soldiers were bribed. No other gospel mentions any of these events. This is astoundingly poor history writing on their part if it all really happened. Also, it is implausible to think no one else would mention a mass resurrection in which "many saints came out of their tombs, went into the holy city and appeared to many" (27:52,53). An incident of that magnitude would have been an amazingly strong support for their cause, and would have verified their message to a great degree.

CHAPTER THREE: OTHER PROBLEMS WITH THE BIBLE

3.1 BOGUS PROPHECIES

I distinctly remember as a child hearing a preacher claim that the odds of Jesus fulfilling all the OT prophecies concerning him are equivalent to filling the entire state of Texas with quarters, marking one, then randomly picking one up and having it be the exact quarter you marked. To this day I have no idea where he got such a preposterous notion.

An authentic prophecy would indeed be an enormous validation for any religion, since everyone knows that being able to predict details of the future is beyond human capability. The problem is there have never been any authentic prophecies, neither in the Bible nor anywhere else. It is certainly true that many OT writings are similar in content to supposed events later in history, yet nowhere are there any cases of prophecies that clearly delineate details that could not possibly be guessed.[29] Scripture, like fortune

---

[29] Daniel chapters 7-12 are often cited by apologists as prophetic, yet they are highly suspect on many levels and perhaps the most spurious in the OT canon as far as authorship and date of composition are concerned. It suffices to say here that they were certainly not written in the sixth century BCE by any single author. The various textual and historical issues of Daniel are beyond the scope of this present study. I refer the reader to any of the

tellers and horoscopes, uses vague language that can be fulfilled by a number of events instead of citing specific names and dates. For example, a truly divine prophecy that no human could produce would be something like the following, if it came true:

> In the year 2037, three nations will form an alliance against the United States. The names of these nations are Russia, Iran, and China. Their leaders will be Dmitry Koslov, Abdul Al-Shareef, and Tuan Wong. They will invade the eastern coast of Maine on July 16 by air and sea, making initial contact at 3:13 Eastern Standard time. After six months of fighting, they will successfully take over Maine, Vermont, New Hampshire, Massachusetts, Connecticut, and Rhode Island, but will advance no further. Their rule in those regions will last until October 14, 2045, when the United States will finalize the recuperation of its lost territories. A total of 556,124 Americans will die as a direct result of the conflict.

Nothing even close to this is in the Bible, yet it would have been incredibly simple for an omniscient god to do. Predicting that a certain army will win a war, that a kingdom will divide, or that a future leader will cause suffering among the populace hardly requires divine foresight.

Not only do numerous prophecies fail to give specific information, many OT passages viewed as prophetic in the NT were never intended to be so by

numerous publications of Hebrew scholars such as John J. Collins and Raymond Hammer.

the original writers. That is to say that early Christians merely found phrases related to an event that supposedly happened in the life of Jesus, then claimed it was a prophecy concerning the Messiah. A good example is Psalm 22, which many read as a foretelling of Christ's crucifixion. Nowhere at all does the original chapter say anything like "Yahweh is revealing what will happen to his Messiah, Jesus, when he is crucified under Pontius Pilate." How was any reader even to know that it was a prophecy? Surely one of the foundational characteristics of foretelling is that it must be clearly stated as such from the beginning. Like the original Psalmist, a number of people have felt alone and abandoned, cursed and persecuted by others. If this is referring specifically to Jesus, why would it not clearly say it? Why are there no names and dates mentioned? The same can be said of Isaiah 53 and other oft-cited chapters in evangelical circles.

It is evident that NT writers like Matthew anxiously attempted to make Jesus fulfill as many so-called prophecies as possible, yet often times failed miserably. As can be seen in the examples below, many of the original texts were not meant to foretell anything at all. The NT authors clearly just combed the text looking for whatever could be related to their current events, then cherry-picked those phrases to claim they were fulfillment of prophecy. This can be done with any book and requires no supernatural ability of any kind. It is equivalent to reading *Moby Dick*, finding a parallel between my life and Ishmael's, then claiming that I fulfill Herman Melville's prophecy. No sensible person would be convinced by such a fatuous assertion.

Richard Carrier, in several of his talks and debates,[30] has pointed out yet another important issue relevant here, namely, that people can fulfill some predictions on their own if they know what they are. If Jesus knew what Psalm 22 said ("My God, my God, why have you forsaken me?"), he could have just quoted it from the cross, like any number of people quote from writings they relate to. If he knew a text predicted the Messiah would ride into Jerusalem on a donkey, he could have simply gotten a donkey and ridden into Jerusalem. That would have required no divine intervention of any sort.

1] Matthew 1:23 maintains that Mary's virgin conception fulfilled Isaiah 7:14.
Although the meaning of the Hebrew word translated "virgin" here is heavily disputed, it did normally refer to a young woman who was sexually pure. Nevertheless, the Isaiah passage still does not make any claim to a miraculous birth but only affirms that "a young woman/virgin will have a child." That is to say, a young woman who was then a virgin would have relations and conceive, which of course would not constitute a miracle. *Nowhere does is declare she would not have relations with anyone, nor that Yahweh would cause the conception* as with Mary in the gospels.

The original passage referred to the real Judean king Ahaz who was under attack from Syria and the northern tribes of Israel when the prophet foretold his military victory. The text later states the boy would be called "Immanuel," and before he knew good and evil, "the land whose two kings you dread" would be deserted" (7:16). That is, *it referred to a*

---

30 Videos are available at www.richardcarrier.info.

baby born in Ahaz' lifetime, not centuries later. Not only was Christ never once called Immanuel in any gospel, what land was deserted before he knew good and evil?

2] Matthew 2:6 adds "by no means" to Micah 5:2.

This goes completely against the supposed prophecy by negating it:

Mic.5:2: Bethlehem...small among the clans of Judah...

Mt.2:6: Bethlehem...*by no means* smallest among the rulers of Judah...

3] Matthew 2:15 asserts that Jesus' flight and return from Egypt fulfilled Hosea 11:1.

After fleeing to Egypt to escape Herod's persecution, Joseph, Mary, and Jesus then allegedly returned to Israel in order to fulfill the prediction that reads "from Egypt I called my son." However, the original verse in Hosea clearly refers to Israel coming out of slavery in Egypt and includes nothing whatsoever about Christ or anything Messianic.

Often theologians will try and classify these as "double prophecies," (one refers to Israel, the second to Jesus),[31] yet such a method essentially means that any two events even slightly resembling each other can be classified as fulfillment of prophecy. As mentioned before, you could do this with any book ever written if you look hard enough.

4] Matthew 2:18 claims Herod's slaughter of infants in Bethlehem fulfilled Jeremiah 31:15.

---

[31] See Strobel's (2000:134,135) interview with Geisler for further explanation.

The original passage of "Rachel weeping for her children" refers to Ramah, which was a town on the way to Babylon during the deportation under Nebuchadnezzar. *It is not even the same city.* Ramah was about five miles north of Jerusalem, while Bethlehem is to the south. This is, of course, a totally separate issue from the event itself, which almost certainly did not occur.[32]

5] Matthew 2:23 declares Jesus moved to Nazareth because "the prophets" said he would "be called a Nazarene."
Even Moody agrees this does not make much sense. The gospel writer might have been trying to do a play on words with the Hebrew for "branch" in Isaiah 11:1, but that verse is certainly not a prophecy about Nazareth. Other possibilities are that he may have been referencing Judges 13:5 and confusing Nazarene with Nazirite (Samson was a Nazirite), or quoting an extra-biblical text. Either way, this passage is simply wrong.

6] In Matthew 12:40, Jesus is said to have prophesied that, like Jonah, "the son of man will be three days and three nights in the heart of the earth."

---

[32] Matthew is the only gospel writer who mentions a massacre in Bethlehem. No other historical record of any kind mentions it either, not even Josephus who wrote extensively on the deeds of Herod. It is very unlikely that Josephus would have chosen to omit such an event from his writings. Even if there were only a few dozen toddlers killed, like many evangelicals propose, it surely would not have escaped attention. The parallel between this slaughter and the one under Pharaoh at the time of Moses' birth also makes Matthew's claims highly suspicious.

According to Matthew himself, Jesus was only in the ground one complete day and two nights. I understand that in ancient Israel a day started at sundown, not midnight, and that any part of a day could be considered a day. However, none of that would explain "three nights."

7] Matthew 21:5-7 claims that Jesus riding two animals into Jerusalem fulfilled a Zechariah 9:9 prophecy.

As was mentioned previously in the contradiction section, the Zechariah passage is poetic alliteration and does not refer to two separate animals. The other gospels do not mention any prophecy related to this event and claim he rode only one animal.

8] Matthew 27:10 proposes that the priests' purchase of a field with 30 pieces of silver fulfilled what "Jeremiah" predicted.

He then quotes a bizarre and convoluted mix of Zechariah 11:12-13, Jeremiah 18, 19, and 32:6-9, none of which say anyone purchased a field for 30 pieces of silver. In chapters 18 and 19, Jeremiah affirms he bought a field, and in chapter 32 he paid "17 shekels." Again, a supernatural fulfillment of prophecy could surely have been a little more precise.

9] Acts 1:20 quotes Psalm 69:25 and 109:8 completely out of context to refer to Judas.

Both of these original passages are imprecatory psalms against David's enemies or "the wicked." In 69:25 and other surrounding verses, both the Hebrew and the Septuagint are *plural*, "may *their* camps be desolate," and therefore refer to more than one person. These chapters also include other petitions in the same context that were not fulfilled at all by Judas, especially 109:15 which states "may memory of them be eliminated." The exact opposite has happened; everyone knows his name and what he did. This is a perfect example of the NT writers cherry-picking "prophecy" from the OT.

10] Acts 2:22-32 references Psalm 16:8-11 as a prediction of Jesus' resurrection.
The main verses emphasized are the following:

> My heart is glad and my tongue rejoices; my body will also rest in hope, because you will not abandon me to the realm of the dead, you will not let your holy one see decay. (New International Version)

There are three difficulties with this passage. First, the original song was composed in Hebrew, and Acts was written in Greek, which means the quote itself is a translation. This causes some significant interpretive issues, the most relevant being the definition of the term translated "realm of the dead" (Hebrew *sheol,* Greek *hades*). Beliefs about these places were diverse and changed over time, but overall it can be said that *sheol* to ancient Jews meant neither "heaven" nor "hell," but rather "the grave," a place where *everyone* would go after they died, whether good or bad. It appears multiple times in the OT as a destination for the righteous (Gen.37:35; Ps.88:3) and the wicked (Num.16:30; Job 21:13; Ps.9:17).

Second, regardless of the meaning of *sheol,* the original context in Psalm 16 clearly demonstrates the author is referring to himself, not Jesus. He openly says "you will not abandon *me,*" not "you will not abandon Jesus (or Messiah, etc.)." Many have interpreted "holy one" to be an allusion to Jesus, yet there is no textual reason to do so. This Hebrew term appears over 30 times in the OT (almost all of them in Psalms) and refers simply to a pious or saintly person. Multiple examples show that other chapters use the word in reference either to the author himself, to king David, or to other believers in Yahweh (Ps.4:3; Ps.18:25; Ps.50:5; Ps.89:19).

The third issue is that the original song makes no mention whatsoever of a *physical* resurrection from the dead *in this world*, which is what the gospels and Acts claim happened with Jesus. The Hebrew literally states "you (Yahweh) will not abandon my *soul* to *sheol*, or let your holy one see corruption." Thus the author affirms it is his "soul" that will not decay after death, and makes no mention of his body. If anything is clear with this passage, it is that the psalmist believes in some sort of afterlife for himself, and that is the extent of what can be satisfactorily defended. As with all the so-called prophecies presented in this section, Psalm 16 is hazy at best and presents the reader with no clear details of any kind, nor does it ever claim to be a prediction of anything related to Jesus.

3.2 REPEATED PASSAGES

Having a double testimony is not a bad thing in itself; in fact, it is normally positive. However, I fail to see the reason for repeating a virtually *identical* passage, especially in the same book. This would make little sense if it were written by the same author and then kept unchanged, but would indeed make perfect sense if it were the work of several human hands who duplicated and edited throughout the centuries. The following are a few examples that appear to have been copied in two different places during the process of compiling the texts together.

1] Exodus 6:10-12 is the same as
Exodus 6:28-30.

2] Exodus 23:19 is the same as
Exodus 34:26.

3] Joshua 15:14-19 is the same as
Judges 1:10-15.

4] Chapters 18-20 of II Kings are the same as
chapters 36-39 of Isaiah, with a few
variations of verse order.

5] Psalm 14 is the same as
Psalm 53, except the addition of an extended
verse 5 in the latter.

6] Psalm 40:13-17 is the same as
Psalm 70:1-5, with a few variations.

7] Proverbs 14:12 is the same as Proverbs
16:25.
8] Proverbs 19:5 is the same as
Proverbs 19:9, except the last phrase "will not
escape" versus "will perish."

9] Proverbs 18:18 is the same as
Proverbs 26:22.

10] Isaiah 2:2-4 is the same as
Micah 4:1-4.

11] Chapters 15 and 16 of Isaiah are the same as Jeremiah 48.

3.3 SCRIBAL CHANGES TO THE NEW TESTAMENT

While there is debate among scholars as to which specific parts of the NT were original and which parts were added for what reason, the fact that there were adjustments of its content is not disputed by any advanced researcher. Some are evident even in the earliest manuscripts, while others were the work of scribes at a much later date.[33] It has been a fluid text, and numerous verses that were once part of the Bible are no longer considered authentic. A simple verification of this is to pick up any recent translation and see if there is a Matthew 17:21, Matthew 23:14, John 5:4, Acts 8:37, or Acts 15:34. In the vast majority, these do not exist anymore, yet when the numbering system was established in the 16th century, they were considered "God's Word." Subsequent discoveries of older Greek manuscripts revealed they were in fact interpolations.

Below are some of the most well-known examples. They clearly demonstrate that the Christian Scripture was not set in stone and handed down

---

[33] Textual Criticism is a fascinating and highly relevant field of study. Nonetheless, a detailed analysis remains beyond the scope of this present book. There have been several quality publications in recent decades by specialists much more qualified than myself. I refer the reader to the titles of Barbara Aland, Kurt Aland, Bart Ehrman, and Bruce Metzger listed in the bibliography.

unchanged over the centuries like so many have believed.[34]

1] Certain scribes changed verses in the gospels in order to better harmonize their content.

A] As was mentioned previously in section 1.5, some scribes added "this class of demon can only come out by prayer and fasting" as Matthew 17:21, since this phrase was absent in Matthew but present in Mark 9:29. Most modern translations acknowledge this and include it only as a footnote.

B] Matthew 19:9 says "whoever divorces his wife, except for immorality, and marries another woman, commits adultery." After this phrase, some scribes also added "and he who marries a divorced woman commits adultery," in order to better harmonize with the message in Mark 10:11,12.

C] Matthew 23:14 ("Woe unto you...for you devour widows' houses....") was added by later scribes to harmonize with Mark 12:40 and Luke 20:47. Most modern versions have acknowledged this and eliminated verse 14 entirely. However, other older but influential translations like the King James have included it.

D] John 20:1 affirms Mary Magdalene left for Jesus' tomb while it was still dark, whereas Mark 16:2 states the sun had already risen. Because of this contradiction, some manuscripts either have the verse in Mark deleted altogether or changed to "while the sun was still rising." Due to the fact that this

---

[34] My main sources for sections 3.3 and 3.4 are Aland et al 2000, Ehrman 2007, and Metzger 2005a. All material presented here can be verified in any number of critical Greek NT publications.

manipulation did not occur in the majority of manuscripts, it is normally not mentioned in modern translations.

2] Matthew 1:16 was tampered with to emphasize the virginity of Mary, Jesus' mother.

For this verse, most manuscripts read something like the following:

> ...Jacob was the father of Joseph, the husband of Mary, of whom was born Jesus who is called Christ.

In some manuscripts (most notably Θ from the 9th century), a copyist has added "the *virgin* Mary," undoubtedly motivated to emphasize the pure and divine conception of Jesus. This reading is also present in some early Latin and Syriac translations.

3] The "Lord's prayer" was edited several times in different ways and the often recited ending was not original to Matthew.

Two gospels include this famous prayer: Matthew and Luke. The textual variants present in the surviving manuscripts are so numerous that it is difficult to sort out. It helps to first view them in a side-by-side comparison, with the bold print showing what is not in Luke:

(New International Version)

MATTHEW 6:9-13	LUKE 11:2-4
Our Father ***in heaven***, hallowed be your name. Your kingdom come, ***your will be done,***	Father, hallowed be your name. Your kingdom come.

on earth as it is in heaven. Give us today our daily bread. And forgive us our ***debts***, as we also have forgiven our ***debtors***. And lead us not into temptation, ***but deliver us from the evil one.***	Give us each day our daily bread. Forgive us our sins, for we also forgive everyone who sins against us. And lead us not into temptation.

Due to the obvious fact that Luke's rendition is quite truncated in comparison, many scribes lengthened it in order to better correspond with Matthew. As is to be expected, most of the additions to Luke are almost identical to Matthew, such as "in heaven" after "Father," "your will be done on earth as it is in heaven," and "deliver us from the evil one." Not all of the interpolations in Luke match with Matthew, however. For instance, a few manuscripts also have "may your Holy Spirit come upon us and cleanse us," a phrase possibly added to more clearly include all members of the Trinity.

Another characteristic that will appear obvious to church goers is the absence of the final phrase "for yours is the kingdom, and the power, and the glory for ever and ever. Amen." Despite its widespread use, this ending is not present in any of the earliest and most authoritative manuscripts of either gospel, and appears to be a later liturgical[35] addition similar in content to David's dedicatory prayer in I Chronicles 29:11-13. It is included in brackets or as a footnote in the majority of modern translations.

---

[35] Something recited during church ceremonies.

4] In Matthew 27:9, some scribes eliminated the name "Jeremiah" in order to hide the author's citation error.

As was previously mentioned in section 3.1, Matthew attributes a prophecy to Jeremiah that is not found in that book and only partially found in Zechariah. Consequently, certain scribes felt the need to amend this mistake in some way, either by changing the name to "Zechariah" or by omitting it altogether.

5] Mark chapter 16 was heavily modified by later scribes, some of which added a short ending and others almost an entire chapter.

What is now Mark 16:9-20 is not in the oldest and most reliable manuscripts. Even conservative scholars admit this, and most modern translations include an explanatory footnote or put these verses in brackets. This section contains the line about "picking up poisonous snakes and not being harmed," a central tenet for the snake handling sects of the Appalachian Mountains. Their entire practice is based on a text that was not even in the original NT.

6] Luke 2:33 was changed in several texts to emphasize that Joseph was not Jesus' biological father.

Referring to Jesus as a child, the earliest manuscripts (including some of the most authoritative like Sinaiticus and Vaticanus) read "his *father* and mother wondered at the words spoken about him." Due to the confusion of parenthood with Joseph, and not wishing to portray Jesus as having an earthly father, certain scribes changed the reading to "*Joseph* and his mother wondered..." in several manuscripts of the 6th through 9th centuries. These modified manuscripts were used to translate the King James and so the latter reading is included in said translation.

7] Luke 22:33-34 about Jesus sweating drops of blood is a later scribal interpolation.

As many critical scholars have pointed out, these verses are not present in the earliest and most reliable manuscripts. Ehrman (2007:164,165) suggests they were likely added due to the fact that Luke does not present Jesus as having gone through any anguish during the trial and crucifixion.

8] John 5:4 about the "angel of the Lord stirring the water" to heal people is not original to the gospel.

The earliest manuscripts do not have this verse. It seems possible it was initially an explanatory side note which eventually came to be considered part of the text itself. As is the case with many other verses here, John 5:4 is recognized as an interpolation in most modern translations, either being relegated to a footnote or kept in brackets.

9] John 7:53-8:11, the famous story about the woman caught in adultery, is a later scribal interpolation.

There is no doubt this story contains an inspiring message with the well-known phrase "let him who is without sin cast the first stone." Nonetheless, the earliest and most reliable manuscripts do not include it, and others have it placed in a different location, such as in Luke. Even conservative scholars agree this story was not original to the gospel of John, yet it continues to be presented as authentic from pulpits throughout the world.

P a g e | **106**

Probably owing to its extremely popular moral lesson, most modern translations include it in brackets with an explanatory footnote, but do not remove it from the main text.

10] Some later scribes added another verse to Acts 8 (later to be verse 37) concerning the baptism of the Ethiopian eunuch.
Baptism was and continues to be a disputed topic among believers of different denominations. A particularly vehement issue has been whether it is required for salvation or not. In every surviving manuscript copied before the 6th century CE, the Ethiopian requests to be baptized in 8:36, then is immediately baptized in the following verse. Likely due to a desire to clarify that baptism alone did not save the Ethiopian, some scribes added what later became verse 37 which included the confession "I believe that Jesus Christ is the Son of God." Most recent versions recognize this interpolation by putting it in brackets or as a footnote.

11] Certain copyists added a verse to Acts 15 in an attempt to clarify the confusing sequence of events.
Due to the fact that Acts 15 implies Silas left Antioch in verses 30-33 yet was still with Paul in Antioch shortly thereafter in verse 40, some thought it necessary to clarify and so added "and it seemed good to Silas to remain there" (i.e. in Antioch) as verse 34. Most recent translations have omitted this verse from the main text, keeping it as a footnote only.

12] Some scribes added that Jesus "resurrected" to Romans 14:9.

In the earliest and most reliable manuscripts, this verse says Jesus "died and lived again." Owing perhaps to certain overzealous scribes' desire to specify exactly what that meant, the verb "resurrected" was later added, with the final result being that "Jesus died, *resurrected*, and lived again." Most modern translations recognize this as an obvious interpolation and so do not include "resurrected."

One could rightfully object that other passages clearly teach Jesus rose from the dead, so such a belief does not stand or fall on this one instance. While this is definitely true, it nevertheless remains a clear example of how the text was manipulated by later copyists according to what they deemed noteworthy.

13] The doxology at the end of Romans 16 is very inconsistently represented in the Greek texts.

There are five distinct options for these verses:
A] Include them as Romans 16:25-27 (the most common).
B] Include them as Romans 14:24-26.
C] Include them as Romans 15:34-36.
D] Include them twice, as both Romans 14:24-26 and Romans 16:25-27.
E] Omit them altogether.

Although the majority of the early and reliable manuscripts include these verses in some place, the variety of locations in which they are found makes them highly suspect. Both Aland et al (2000) and Metzger (2005a) admit the possibility of them being an interpolation not original to Paul's epistle. Some modern versions like the English Standard and New International acknowledge this issue in a footnote, but do not remove the verses or put them in brackets.

14] Some later texts of I Timothy 3:16 call Jesus "God," while others do not.

Speaking of Jesus, the earliest manuscripts say "...*who* appeared in the flesh..." while many later ones have "...*God* appeared in the flesh..."

Whether this particular case was intentional or not is uncertain, but it is included here due to its theological significance. It could possibly have been accidental, since the Greek word for "god" was often abbreviated as two letters ΘC, which were very similar to the relative pronoun OC "who." The most reliable early texts all have the relative OC "who," but several later texts have it as ΘC "god." In fact, in a few early manuscripts such as Alexandrinus, a later copyist actually added "god" in the line above "who" (Ehrman 2007:157).

The divinity of Jesus is certainly taught in other passages, so the doctrine is not unique to this one verse. Nevertheless, it is an interesting example of how the message of these texts can be changed quite easily, even if it is not intentional.

15] I John 5:7,8 was manipulated to make the idea of the Trinity more clearly taught in Scripture.

The earliest and most reliable Greek manuscripts read "there are three that witness, the spirit, the water, and the blood." Due to the hazy nature of this phrase, a few later manuscripts from the 15th and 16th centuries changed it to read "there are three that witness in heaven: the Father, the Son, and the Spirit. And these three are one and they witness on the earth." To their credit, most modern translations have rectified this by removing these additions from the main text.

3.4 SORTING THROUGH
THE TEXTUAL VARIANTS

When reading a modern translation of the Bible, few people realize they are reading an edited work. In other words, a group of scholars has examined the Hebrew and Greek manuscripts and decided which textual variants should be in the final version and which should not. We must remember there is no singular "biblical text" but rather multiple "texts." This is particularly so for the NT. Many copies have survived and those copies are *not* the same. In certain passages, we simply cannot tell what the original author wrote, so the translators must pick through the variants and decide which is the preferred reading. This is no easy task and there is often disagreement even among the experts. Although there are many legitimate criteria for their decisions, often times they must be subjective.

Few Christians realize there are literally hundreds of variants between the manuscripts, and at times they significantly change the nuances the verses convey. The most common differences are seen in individual words, which at times are even complete opposites. In such cases, (particularly in #2, #9, #10, #11, and #15 below) the Greek manuscripts themselves directly contradict one another.

Ultimately, then, it is a translation committee who decides what the Bible says in such cases. There is no voice from the heavens dictating the final product; it is human from start to finish. Humans write it, humans copy it, humans change it, humans edit it, and humans translate it. At no step along the way is there any measurable divine intervention.

What follows will serve to give the reader a taste of the problems that arise when attempting to sort through the available manuscripts to produce a modern translation. The bold italicized words are all legitimate variants that can be confirmed in any critical version of the Greek NT. The reading preferred by the majority of committees is presented first, but they are not agreed on by all.

1] Matthew 19:29

a] "Whoever has left houses...children, or fields for my sake will receive **100 times** in return..."
b] "Whoever has left houses...**wife**, children, or fields for my sake will receive **100 times** in return..."
c] "Whoever has left houses...children, or fields for my sake will receive **many times** in return..."

2] Matthew 21:31

(Jesus speaks of two sons. The first says he will obey his father but does not do it, the second says he will not obey but later does.)
a] "Which of the two did his father's will? ...the *first*."
b] "Which of the two did his father's will? ...the *last*."[36]

3] Matthew 24:36

a] "No one knows the day or the hour, not even the angels in heaven **nor the Son** (i.e. Jesus), but the Father alone."
b] "No one know the day or the hour, not even the angels in heaven, but the Father alone."

---

[36] These verses contain additional variants that are quite complicated to present in this format. I recommend the reader to Metzger (2005a) for a more thorough explanation.

4] John 6:69

(Peter replies to Jesus. Christ = Messiah.)

a] "We have believed and know that you are the *holy one of God*."

b] "We have believed and know that you are the *Christ,* the *holy one of God*."

c] "We have believed and know that you are the *Christ,* the *Son of God*."

d] "We have believed and know that you are the *Christ,* the *Son of the living God*."

5] John 8:38

(Jesus speaks to those who do not believe in him.)

a] "...you do the things which you have *heard* from *the* Father."

b] "...you do the things which you have *heard* from *your* Father."

c] "...you do the things which you have *seen* from *the* Father."

d] "...you do the things which you have *seen* from *your* Father."

6] John 9:4

(Jesus speaks to his disciples.)

a] "*We* must do the works of him who sent *me*..."

b] "*We* must do the works of him who sent *us*..."

c] "*I* must do the works of him who sent *me*..."

7] John 13:10

a] "He who has bathed does not need to wash, **except his feet**."

b] "He who has bathed does not need to wash *his head*, *except his feet alone*."

c] "He who has bathed does not need to wash."

8] Acts 5:3

(Peter speaks to someone who lied to him.)
a] "Why has Satan *filled* your heart...?"
b] "Why has Satan *injured* your heart...?"
c] "Why has Satan *tempted* your heart...?"

9] Acts 12:25

a] "Paul and Barnabus returned *from* Jerusalem..."
b] "Paul and Barnabus returned *to* Jerusalem...."
c] "Paul and Barnabus returned *out of* Jerusalem..."
d] "Paul and Barnabus returned *from* Jerusalem *to Antioch*..."

10] Romans 4:19

a] "[Abraham]...*considered* his own body as dead, being 100 years old..."
b] "[Abraham]...*did not consider* his own body as dead, being 100 years old..."

11] I Corinthians 15:51

a] "We will *not* all *sleep* (i.e. die), but we will all *be changed*."
b] "We will all *sleep*, but we will *not* all *be changed*."
c] "We will *not* all *sleep*, and we will *not* all *be changed*."

12] Galatians 5:22,23

a] "The fruit of the Spirit is...self-control."
b] "The fruit of the Spirit is...self-control, *and purity*."
c] "The fruit of the Spirit is...self-control, *and perseverance*."

13] Colossians 1:12
a] "...giving thanks to the Father who has *qualified you*..."
b] "...giving thanks to *God* the Father who has *qualified us*..."
c] "...giving thanks to the Father who has *called us*..."
d] "...giving thanks to the Father who has *qualified and called you*..."

14] I Timothy 4:10
a] "For this reason we labor and *exert ourselves*..."
b] "For this reason we labor and *suffer reproach*..."

15] II Peter 3:10
a] "...the earth and the things in it will *be found/exposed*."
b] "...the earth and the things in it will *be burned*."
c] "...the earth and the things in it will *disappear*."
d] "...the earth and the things in it will *be found destroyed*."

16] Revelation 13:18
(The author speaks of the "mark of the beast.")
a] "...and his number is *666*."
b] "...and his number is *616*."

The second reading of this extremely popular verse is present in a minority of manuscripts, but some are from as early as the 4th century CE. Metzger (2005a) claims it possibly was meant to refer to Emperor Nero, with each letter in his name representing a number, all of which together formed 666 or 616. If the Greek spelling of his name was used (Nero*n*), the letters would equal 666; if the Roman spelling was used, it would be 616.

CONCLUSION

The presence of such discrepancies makes perfect sense if we take the Bible as a human book imperfectly written, copied, and edited over centuries. Numerous authors in different times and places were bound to make mistakes and disagree with each other, and the same is true for virtually any ancient text compiled and copied in such a way for so long a time. Their existence should therefore come as no surprise.

However, one might reasonably ask how it is possible for so many problems to go unnoticed in a book that has been read by so many followers for centuries. The main reason, in my opinion based on years in the church, is simply that most Christians do not actually study the Bible to any significant degree. These inconsistencies and flaws only appear through strenuous examination of the details, and by painstakingly comparing one passage with another, often times in the original languages. Needless to say, most believers are not interested in that. They are content to peruse their favorite passages in their favorite translation and never do anything more. There is really no nice way to put it; the average Christian is intellectually lazy and embarrassingly ignorant. The vast majority have never read a single book on Church History, Textual Criticism, Theology, Biology, Psychology, biblical languages, or other religions. Their beliefs are a nice little get-out-of-hell-free card that makes them feel good about death and suffering in this life, and they simple do not care to examine it at any greater depth. They go to church to sing songs, hear an inspiring message, and talk to their friends. That's about it.

When faced with the specific problems analyzed here, most will react in a number of ways, depending on the person. The conservative scholars will merely continue affirming inerrancy for the original manuscripts and brush the discrepancies aside as copyist errors. As was argued earlier, such a claim is totally meaningless since we do not actually have any original manuscripts. It is equivalent to me declaring that my imaginary friend is bigger and stronger than anyone else's.

Nothing can be said to those fundamentalists who continue contending inerrancy, denying that contradictions exist at all. They are textbook definitions of closed minds, impossible to persuade regardless of evidence presented. They hold to the unfalsifiable inerrancy mentioned in the introduction and their statements are as empty as any other religious group claiming to have a perfect revelation from a perfect god. They obviously are making a desperate attempt to hold on to cherished beliefs in the face of legitimate scriptural problems.

Religious conservatives, like many people, cannot stand the idea that what they have believed their whole life just may be wrong, so they go to great lengths to convince themselves of their baseless doctrines. The difference between me and them is that when I realized the evidence was against me, *I changed my beliefs.* I went where the evidence led whether I liked it or not, yet they stick to their dogma at all cost. They push skeptics like me aside as people who are "just bitter," or who have an axe to grind, or are living in sin and blinded by the Devil.

Not all Christians are closed minded, however. There are a great deal of genuine and respectful believers who truly think the Bible can be the "Word of God" despite all its mistakes. They argue that the details do not matter and that none of the discrepancies I have presented really affect any vital doctrine. Yet if Yahweh is only concerned with the main points of his message and not all the secondary minutiae, then what is the point of "revealing" them? Why not just leave them out altogether? Detailed lists comprise countless chapters in the Bible, all painstakingly copied by hand for more than a millennium. If they are not important, why are they there in the first place?

There is still another group of believers who not only will acknowledge the discrepancies but will actually view them as a positive aspect of Scripture. They believe the overall lessons are what count and the existence of mistakes and morally questionable doctrines demonstrate how Yahweh used human imperfection to communicate his message. Such people are at least honest in acknowledging the evidence, for which I am grateful, but are still making unfalsifiable assertions that have no advantage over any other religious faith. On what basis could they claim that Mormonism and Islam are wrong, then? To me, it seems ludicrous that a personal god who really wants to get his or her message across would do so by using stories that are not actually true and by mandating activities that are damaging to society (such as polygamy and slavery). Why would such a god not have spoken clearly to all from the beginning, in all languages? Why would we need to translate or copy anything at all? Imagine how convincing it would have been if the American Indians and Chinese had all received the same message of Jesus, and when missionaries showed up, they had responded "well, we already knew all of that!"

It appears, then, that many believers genuinely do not care about evidence. Religion gives them meaning and fulfillment and whether or not science and history validate the data is irrelevant. Some, however, do care a great deal about evidence when they think it supports their Scripture. When certain historical or archaeological discoveries coincide with something mentioned in the Bible (which, of course, means nothing in regard to their theological claims), they will announce such data as proof they were right all along. Yet when you corner them with evidence against a scriptural teaching, they back up and say "well, it's not that important, really. The main message of love and salvation is not affected by minor discrepancies in the text."

This type of picking and choosing commonly occurs as well when the topic is evolution. I have personally held arguments about scientific evidence with Christians who, after they have run out of a defense, will conclude that "this issue really isn't that important to me. Whether Genesis is literally true or not isn't as central as the message of Jesus." So it appears that evidence is important to them only when it is in their favor.

The fundamental problem is that people are making extraordinary claims without extraordinary evidence. The Bible is not inerrant, perfect, nor wholly reliable, as the presented data clearly indicates. An almighty god would not have the slightest trouble writing a text that was clear and harmonious. That is just not what we have, plain and simple. Being good is not enough; it needs to be great. Humans can do a good job themselves without divine help. To say the Bible is flawless and is the only god's word to mankind is an incredibly extraordinary claim. Such an assertion without doubt requires extraordinary evidence. The information examined here shows conclusively that Scripture fails to be anything like that, and is a far cry from a perfect book.

All that being said, there is no denying that the Bible is a fundamental text of Western civilization and contains many inspirational messages and literary wonders. I am in no way suggesting that we throw it out, in fact, quite the opposite. I strongly encourage everyone to read it thoroughly and see for themselves the good and the bad. Read the Bible, by all means, but read all of it and in detail.

Bibliography and suggestions for further reading

Books on biblical studies

Aland, Barbara et al (eds.). *The Greek New Testament* (4th revised ed.). Deutsche Bibelgesellschaft. 2000.

Aland, Kurt and Barbara Aland. *The Text of the New Testament: An Introduction to the Critical Editions and to the Theory and Practice of Modern Textual Criticism* (2nd ed.). Eerdmans. 1995.

Barker, Dan. *God: the most unpleasant character in all of fiction*. Sterling. 2016.

Burr, William Henry. *Self-contradictions in the Bible*. Prometheus Books. 1987 (originally published in 1859).

Carrier, Richard. *On the Historicity of Jesus: Why We Might Have Reason for Doubt*. Sheffield Phoenix Press. 2014.

Comfort, Phillip (ed.). *Origin of the Bible*. Tyndale House. 2013.

Copan, Paul. *Is God a Moral Monster? Making sense of the Old Testament*. Baker Books. 2011.

Craig, William Lane. *Reasonable Faith: Christian Truth and Apologetics*. Crossway. 2008.

Ehrman, Bart. *Lost Christianities*. Oxford. 2005.

Ehrman, Bart. *Misquoting Jesus*. HarperOne. 2007.

Ehrman, Bart. *Jesus, Interrupted*. HarperOne. 2009.

Ehrman, Bart. *How Jesus became God*. HarperOne. 2014.

Finkelstein, Israel and Neil Asher Silberman. *The Bible Unearthed: Archaeology's New Vision of Ancient Israel and the Origin of Its Sacred Texts*. Touchstone. 2002.

Friedman, Richard. *Who wrote the Bible?* HarperOne. 1987.

Geisler, Norman and Thomas Howe. *The Big Book of Bible Difficulties: Clear and Concise Answers from Genesis to Revelation*. Baker Books. 2008.

Gottwald, Norman K. *The tribes of Yahweh: a sociology of the religion of liberated Israel, 1250–1050 BCE.* Continuum International Publishing. 1999.

Halpern, Bruce. *David's Secret Demons: Messiah, Murderer, Traitor, King.* Eerdmans. 2004.

Hayes, Christine. *Introduction to the Bible.* Yale University Press. 2012.

Hurmence Green, Ruth. *A Born Again Skeptic's Guide to the Bible.* Freedom from Religion Foundation. 1999.

Loftus, John (ed.). *The Christian Delusion: why faith fails.* Prometheus Books. 2010.

Loftus, John (ed.). *Christianity is not Great: how faith fails.* Prometheus Books. 2014.

McDowell, Josh and Sean McDowell. *The Bible Handbook of Difficult Verses: A Complete Guide to Answering the Tough Questions.* Harvest House Publishers. 2013.

Metzger, Bruce. *The Canon of the New Testament: its Origin, Development, and Significance.* Clarendon Press. 1997.

Metzger, Bruce. *A Textual Commentary on the Greek New Testament.* Hendrickson. 2005a.

Metzger, Bruce. *The Text of the New Testament: Its Transmission, Corruption, and Restoration* (4th ed.). Oxford. 2005b.

Miller, Stephen M. and Robert V. Huber. *The Bible: A History. The Making and Impact of the Bible.* Good Books. 2004.

Paget, James Carleton and Joachim Schaper (eds.). *The New Cambridge History of the Bible*, volumes 1-3. Cambridge. 2012-2016.

Paine, Thomas. *The Age of Reason.* CreateSpace Independent Publishing. 2015 (originally published in 1807).

Rydelnik, Michael, Michael Vanlaningham (eds.), et al. *Moody Bible Commentary.* Moody Publishers. 2014.

Strobel, Lee. *The Case for Faith.* Zondervan. 2000.

Wells, Steve. *The Skeptic's Annotated Bible.* SAB Books. 2013.

Books on non-belief or leaving the faith

Barker, Dan. *Godless*. Ulysses Press. 2008.

Carrier, Richard. *Why I am not a Christian*. Philosophy Press. 2011.

Dawkins, Richard. *The God Delusion*. Mariner Books. 2008.

Everett, Daniel. *Don't Sleep, There are Snakes: Life and Language in the Amazonian Jungle*. Vintage. 2009.

Hirsi Ali, Ayaan. *Infidel*. Atria Books. 2008.

Hitchens, Christopher (ed.). *The Portable Atheist*. Da Capo Press. 2007.

Hitchens, Christopher. *God is not Great: How Religion Poisons Everything*. Twelve. 2009.

Hume, David. *An Enquiry Concerning Human Understanding*. CreateSpace Independent Publishing. 2013 (originally published in 1748).

Mills, David. *Atheist Universe*. Ulysses Press. 2006.

Navabi, Armin. *Why there is no god*. CreateSpace Independent Publishing. 2014.

Russell, Bertrand. *Why I am not a Christian and Other Essays on Religion and Related Subjects*. Touchstone. 1967.

Templeton, Charles. *Farewell to God: My Reasons for Rejecting the Christian Faith*. McClelland & Stewart. 1999.

Warraq, Ibn. *Why I am not a Muslim*. Prometheus Books. 1995.

Books on evolution written for deniers

Coyne, Jerry. *Why evolution is true*. Penguin Books. 2009.

Dawkins, Richard. *Evolution: the greatest show on earth*. Free Press. 2010.

Nye, Bill. *Undeniable: Evolution and the Science of Creation*. St. Martin's Griffin. 2015.

Prothero, Donald. *Evolution: what the fossils say and why it matters*. Columbia University Press. 2007.

Prothero, Donald. *The Story of Life in 25 fossils*. Columbia
    University Press. 2015.

Websites

atheistscholar.org
debunkingchristianity.blogspot.com
ffrf.org
infidels.org
patheos.com
richarddawkins.net
skepticsannotatedbible.com
studybible.info
unbound.biola.edu

Made in United States
North Haven, CT
27 March 2023

34607154R00075